BOOK OF TARTS

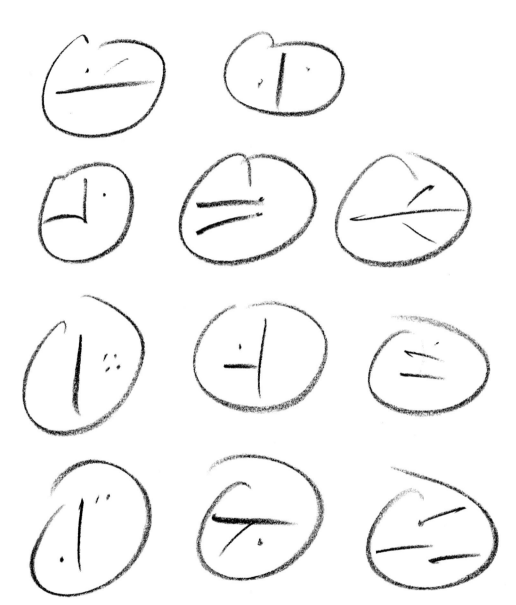

BOOK

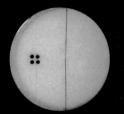

OF TARTS

Form, Function, and Flavor at The City Bakery

MAURY RUBIN

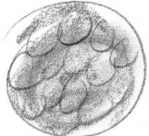

Photographs by
CHRIS CALLIS

William Morrow and Company, Inc. New York

To my mother and father

It is the policy of William Morrow and Company, Inc.,
and its imprints and affiliates, recognizing the impor-
tance of preserving what has been written, to print the
books we publish on acid-free paper, and we exert our
best efforts to that end.

Library of Congress Cataloging-in-Publication Data

Rubin, Maury.

Book of tarts : form, function, and flavor at The City
Bakery / Maury Rubin.

    p.   cm.

Includes index.

ISBN 0-688-12254-X

1. Pies. 2. City Bakery (New York, N.Y.)   I. Title.

TX773.R83   1995

641.8'652—dc20   94–32734
                                    CIP

Printed in the United States of America

First Edition

1 2 3 4 5 6 7 8 9 10

BOOK DESIGN BY 4M'S

ACKNOWLEDGMENTS

Jane Orans championed me first, and wonderful things have come from her friendship and enduring support. Jeff Louis has been another great supporter and friend. For Jeff, I maintain that this book will remain a holiday gift-giving option for years to come. Doug Kreeger, Rick Beckwitt, Don Schatz, and Bob Zises each helped City Bakery get off the ground.

Thanks to Gerard Seurre, whose patisserie in Paris is where I first baked, and to Denis Ruffel for introducing me to Monsieur Seurre. In New York, the influence of Greenmarket has been vital to me. Thanks especially to Eleanor Cole, Vince D'Attolico, Chip Kent, Elizabeth Ryan, Barry Benepe, and Jay and Joel, the estimable Patraker brothers.

Special thanks to literary agent David Black, a real pro, who helped me accomplish the things I cared about. There was valuable effort, encouragement, and advice from Rose Levy Beranbaum, Jackie Bobrow, Michael Capotosto, Alberta Testanero, Merideth Harte, Leslie Goldman, Stephen Pevner, Gene O'Connell, and Ed Braverman. Thanks to MaryAnne Kuzniar, who listened with the patience of ten men to endless hours of book-talk. My brother Barry, who listened to many endless hours himself, was there with support and advice as always.

In putting the book together, three people have meant the most to me. Michael Kaye, one of my favorite talents, put his neck on the line because he cared so much and so well for me to get the book I wanted. His help let me walk away still breathing. Lauri Feldman, daughter of Chicago, made me write. She focused me, led me to the truth of my own thoughts, and helped me put them on paper. Because of Lauri, the book has weight. And because of Chris Callis, the nicest guy in the world, this book has photographs that are right-on and beautiful, and make the book something I'll always treasure. Besides the great pictures, through nearly two years of work, Chris was patient, selfless, enlightening, and a friend. Thanks also to Chris's staff, especially Barry, Lance, John, and Lauren, for so much help.

Lastly, I want to acknowledge the staff at City Bakery, past and present, who have worked their hearts out to help build the bakery. This group makes me enormously proud, and I will always be grateful to them, especially Penka Slavova, Ludmilla Biderman, Rosario Apolinar, Juan B. Landi, Camilo Apolinar, John McCormick, Bridget Conry, Valentin Hernandez, Bernard Galarza, Stephanie Freund, Eric Cohen, Carol Austin, Jamie Owen, and Sarah Squire. And though he's gone from City Bakery, a final thank you to Daniel Zambrelli, my one and only pastry hero. I think about him often when I bake, and I suppose I always will.

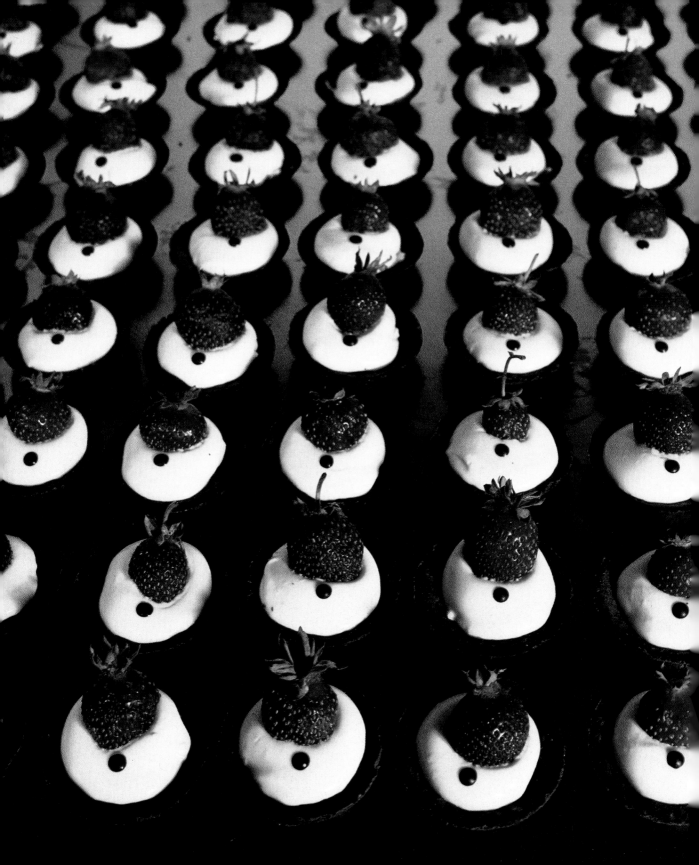

CONTENTS

THE ROAD TO CITY BAKERY

I guess I should start at the beginning: Pop-Tarts. In spite of my mother's home baking, Kellogg's Pop-Tarts were the formative pastry of my youth. From as early as I can remember, I ate a Pop-Tart nearly every day of my childhood—and well into my teens. Frightening as this calculation may be, it's no exaggeration to say that during that period, I ingested nearly three thousand of them. Dutch Apple, Blueberry, and Brown Sugar Cinnamon were staples. Concord Grape, with its distinctive purple inside and white frosted outside, was an alternate.

How this experience led me to a career as a pastry chef, I'm not sure. I am willing to give Kellogg's partial credit. Beyond that, it's my view that chance, obsession, and some American enterprise each played a role.

I moved to New York City in 1982 to work in television at ABC Sports. I had been hired as an assistant to the producer on a new show with Howard Cosell. New York: the art, the architecture, Broadway, Central Park. But none of these impressed me as much as the enormous variety of food. I began to think a lot about the food.

With the assistance of a corporate expense account, I began eating very well and, as a result, selectively. Then I began traveling, and I started concentrating on developing story ideas that were in cities with restaurants that I had read about and wanted to try. (Only now, years removed from ABC's accountants, can I reveal that it was no coincidence that I traveled to San Francisco so many times.) On the road, I was looking for the best meal I could find, no matter what city I was in. At home in New York, but with no time to cook, I got hooked reading cookbooks. I became a lunchtime regular at the New York Public Library branch on West Fifty-third Street, where I'd sit in the stacks reading cookbooks. I was especially intrigued by the recipes of Madeleine Kamman and the philosophy of Alice Waters at Chez Panisse.

At the 1984 Summer Olympics in Los Angeles, my assignment was to cover potential terrorist acts that threatened to interrupt the Games. Fortunately, none took place. As a result, I spent three weeks driving all over LA, eating at restaurants from a list I had written before the Olympics began. I have fond memories of ginger crème brûlée at Chinois on Main, of authentic Mexican food in East LA, of sitting on the deck drinking date shakes at The Source on Sunset Boulevard. Thank goodness the terrorists stayed away. After the Olympics, I was even more preoccupied with eating and cooking. I spent a year in this frame of mind, then decided on a change. In June 1986, I left television, and moved to Paris.

I signed up for a six-day pastry course near Lyons. The instructor was Denis Ruffel, pastry chef of Pâtisserie Millet in Paris, a man possessed by pastry. Through his classes, I saw how creative a medium pastry making could be. When the course ended, I told the chef that I would be staying in France and wanted to learn more about pastry. He offered to help, and he arranged for me to apprentice in a pastry shop in Paris.

Rousseau-Seurre Pâtisserie is at 22 rue des Martyrs, in the 9th Arrondissement. It's not one of the famous pastry shops in Paris. It's a family business whose reputation, like many French pâtisseries, does not extend beyond its quarter. The kitchen staff numbered three: dough man, cake man, and all-purpose pastry man. Gerard Seurre, the owner and chef, spent little time in the kitchen. He was, however, concerned about my education, and made sure that I learned each station. Part of the routine of French kitchens is teaching, and each worker shared the responsibility for teaching me. I began with no knowledge or experience with pastry, so I had no reference point for how much I was learning. But as time passed, I realized that I was receiving a great education: The pastry was made in the classic manner. The work was intense and hands-on. It was the first time in my life that I enjoyed manual labor.

I moved from Rousseau-Seurre to Robert Linxe's La Maison du Chocolat, famous for its handmade chocolates. The kitchen was referred to as the "laboratory," and it was not a pleasant place to be. It was just before Christmas and there was a new chef. The mood was uptight and no one made an effort to teach me. I wasn't given the opportunity to work *with* the chocolate so much as I was allowed the privilege to be *around* the chocolate. Even so, my time at Maison was valuable. I learned quality control of the highest standard, and I stored away some chocolate ideas for later on.

These two apprenticeships, which lasted not quite five months, were the basis of my education. I also spent two weeks making pastry in a small restaurant where I had enjoyed a meal and asked the chef if I could work in his kitchen. After that, I went back to Denis Ruffel at Pâtisserie Millet. There were no openings in the kitchen, but he offered me the chance simply to stand and watch. Millet is a great pastry shop, and I was more than satisfied to get the exposure.

When I returned from Paris after seven months, I couldn't wait to try every bakery in New York. When I did, the realization came fast: New York City didn't have great bakeries. Compared to Paris, the pastry didn't rate. But it wasn't only by the French standard that New York pastry failed me. By an improving American standard of cuisine, it fell short. The approach to ingredients and aesthetics was old school: canned fruits, gelatin cakes, icing decorations six inches deep. These baked goods weren't just average, they were behind the food times.

I took a job in an Upper East Side "French" pastry shop. This was the first in a series of job disasters: one bakery after another where the work situation failed because I didn't believe in the quality. I knew I could do better, and I began dreaming of my own bakery.

I wanted to apply a "Chez Panissian" approach of local foods and seasonal menus to a bakery. Organic flours, eggs from free-range chickens, dairy products and fruits from nearby farms. And I wanted to show that traditional French pastry could be reimagined through an American perspective and become unique—especially in terms of design. I wanted to breathe life into the basic idea of what an American bakery could be.

I spent the next two years developing recipes and looking for possible investors. But bakeries, I learned, were not hot investment properties. A lot of time passed. The waiting, however, served me well; the food ideas grew up in my mind and a better vision of the bakery emerged.

The City Bakery opened in December 1990. Since that time, its reputation has come to be based largely on its tarts. Developing these ideas over the past few years has been the focus of my creative energy. Now, hundreds of recipe requests later, I'm happy to share my methods for making them.

MAURY RUBIN
New York City

ABOUT THE TARTS

A Simple Craft The notion of pastry as an exacting discipline is overrated. The more I learn about pastry, the more I find that ingredients *are* forgiving, that the process *does* allow for occasional minor mistakes. Sure, pastry making can be elevated to the level of art, but, practically speaking, it's craft. There are two basic requirements: an environment that minimizes the possibility of mistakes and measuring accurately. Beyond that, patience and organization matter as much as anything. Confidence helps too.

Trust These Recipes They are straightforward and not technically demanding. If complicated recipes made better pastry, I'd write very complicated ones. In the period before City Bakery opened, one of my main concerns was to develop recipes that were simple enough to be taught to, and quickly absorbed by, new employees. As a result, you will find that all the recipes in this book are made by one of a few basic methods. For example, the cream and sugar coating used for Blueberry-Coconut Tart is also used for a grape tart, apple tart, pear tart, and fig tart. Several chocolate tarts follow the same technique. If you learn the few basic techniques, you can make every tart in the book.

Follow the instructions, but don't obsess. I know the feeling of being a slave to cookbook instructions: working in slow motion, twisting your neck around to read the same line ten times before actually doing anything. Believe me, that's not necessary. Devote your energy instead to refining your execution and being enterprising with the food.

In Praise of Good Ingredients Use of local ingredients has become popular for restaurants in recent years, but not for bakeries. Many restaurants today even have backyard gardens where they grow herbs and lettuces, sometimes even fruits and vegetables. We've followed that lead. Our "garden" is a parking lot down the street called the Union Square Greenmarket. Four days out of every week small farmers from the region turn this lot into one of great open-air food markets in the country. Here's where we find the exceptional fruits that we use for tarts, as well as the vegetables for our lunch menu. The New York, New Jersey, Pennsylvania region is an agriculturally rich one, and through the Greenmarket, we have access to the best of it. We choose fruits of each season that are literally only hours out of the fields and orchards. Raspberries on the bush one night are in City Bakery tarts the next morning. Working in this manner, so close to the source, has many rewards. Foremost to a city chef is that working with local farmers offers a connection to the land. You learn more about food from talking with farmers than from any other means. And farmers are giving. On occasion they've asked me if I'd like to have something special grown. A particular berry? A new variety of melon? This offer of earth from a farmer is the best compliment a chef can receive.

From the sublime to the ordinary, every ingredient counts. For a run-down of basic ingredients see page 8.

Tired Design The psyche of traditional pastry design seems to be without reason. Bakeries do what they do with design and they do it for a long time. Look into the window of any bakery and you'll recognize the same pastries you've always known. Of course this isn't all bad. Seeing the same old cakes and pastries is part of what makes one's favorite bakery seem like an old friend. But pleasing the tradition-bound pastry lover is not the only reason bakeries produce the same goods year after year. The truth is, American bakers are in a creative rut. For lack of either inspiration or ability, pastry design as an evolving part of the bakery process has collapsed in bakeries. Over time, surely this has damaged the bakery as an institution. Baked goods need not be redesigned each year like automobiles, but they are, nonetheless, a retail product competing in the marketplace like any other. Perhaps if the neighborhood American bakery had some creative verve, it would not have become nearly extinct. The fact is, the bakery in this country has traveled the sorry path from being a fixture on Main Street to just another section in the local supermarket. Is this not cause for action? Why should we not expect some tradition *and* creative energy from a bakery? Why, when fields such as film, dance, theater, fashion, architecture, music, and even cooking get a new creative charge each season, have bakers and bakeries sat idle for so long?

Pastry-bag Mania Part of the problem may be the pastry bag. A standard piece of equipment in most bakeries, a pastry bag is a triangular-shaped piece of nylon with a hole in one end to accommodate a pastry tip. Through this tip, ingredients such as chocolate, whipped cream, and those nasty artificially colored gels are piped on top of pastries for design. There's the star tip, the rosette tip, and for devotees of traditional French pastry, there's the St. Honoré tip. Ooh-la-la! The problem is that while everyone uses pastry bags for design, no one is creating new pastry tips. If you're a traditionalist and like a flourish of roses upon your cake, this may pose no conflict. But if you prefer a design that goes beyond Victorian, you're stuck. In a way, pastry chefs don't even really design cakes anymore, they just choose which pastry tip to use. It's time for pastry chefs to develop their own pastry tips and have them manufactured; then they can produce some new pastry designs.

When I apprenticed in France, I watched the process of design sink repeatedly under its own excess. First, a cake was dusted with cocoa powder - a clean look. Then chocolate shavings were added. Then the pastry bag came out: Now dark chocolate doodles circled the whole affair. I'd clench my teeth and shout to myself, "Enough!" It wasn't until white chocolate shavings topped the whole thing off that the cake was left alone.

Lines and Dots To me, pastry design is about discipline. With a tart or cake before you, it can be hard to resist adding just one more decorative touch here and another there, before it's gone too far. As a result, pastry design is often driven less by the intention to create something beautiful than by the inability to resist showing off one's technical skills (with a pastry bag).

At The City Bakery, part of what a design is is what it's *not*. A single chocolate line drawn across a tart creates a design, but because it is so spare, its greater impact seems to be as a marker that the rest of the tart is bare. Most of our tarts have a single line and a few dots juxtaposed in geometric patterns (see page 24). The aesthetic actually has as much to do with form as it does with decoration. For example, I borrowed an idea from the work of architect Frank Lloyd Wright to create Passion Fruit Tart with a Raspberry Polka Dot. Wright said that a house should be "of the hill, not on it." That concept was applied to a tart by building the raspberry polka dot into the passion fruit cream from bottom to top. Consequently, what is structural is also decorative. That's form and function in the pastry kitchen.

Spontaneity of Design In developing fruit tarts, we've moved beyond the realm of the mint leaf garnish. Fruits are arranged randomly on every tart. Spontaneity informs composition. When you assemble fruit tarts at home, forget what you've seen in cookbooks and bakeries. Create a pastry as if you've never seen one before. Arrange fruits upside down, sideways, or inside out. How can you do that? Try using kitchen hand tools in ways for which they aren't intended. For example, muskmelon in a Geometric State of Mind was created after putting an apple corer through a melon, which produced unusual but perfect columns of fruit. Shaved Honeydew with Blackberries came from experimenting with a vegetable peeler on the *inside* of a fruit instead of on the outside.

There are no rules in creating design. If you have a creative impulse, use it. No cookbook gods are staring over your shoulder in the kitchen, ready to strike if you try something new or bizarre.

Basic Ingredients

The foundation of a bakery is the quality of its milk, cream, butter, eggs, and flour. We're always looking for the best.

Heavy Cream More than any other ingredient in these tarts, it's cream that's worth a special search. Truly farm-fresh cream—thick and unctuous, with a taste that says "barn," in a good way—will dramatically enhance the quality of the tarts. Unfortunately, as the small American dairy farm edges closer to extinction, truly farm-fresh cream is harder and harder to find. Even in New York, the third largest dairy-producing state in the country, supplies of high-quality cream are inconsistent. How to find great cream? If you live near a university, try calling the agricultural school. Often, its staff works with small farmers in the region and will be aware of the distribution of regional dairy sources. If, like most people, however, you buy cream in a supermarket, compare the taste of different brands, and always check dates for the freshest.

Butter I long for a small New York State butter producer to show up at the door of City Bakery. Of course, the fate of butter follows the fate of good cream, leaving us to rely on commercial brands. Use unsalted butter, and be sure it tastes and smells fresh.

Milk These recipes use whole milk. If possible, buy milk that is free of rBGH, a synthetic hormone. If the label does not specify—dairy companies are not obligated to do so—ask.

Eggs These recipes use large eggs. Buy eggs that come from free-range chickens.

Flour Flour is where my belief in organic farming began. We use only organic flour, and I care greatly about the fact that the many tons of flour we use in a year leave behind healthy soil. The flour that we use for the tart dough is an unbleached all-purpose white flour, without germ. Look for organic flours at health food stores; sometimes it can be hard to find an organic white flour with the germ removed. Regular unbleached, all-purpose white flour works perfectly in these tarts.

Chocolate I'm loyal to Valrhona, a French brand that at present has only limited retail availability in America. It has style, it's subtle and smooth, and I like the way the flavor takes its time to come through. When you shop for chocolate, taste different brands; chocolate from two different companies can be of equal quality but taste entirely different—lean, smoky, fruity, or bitter. One way to arrive at a unique chocolate flavor is to combine different brands in the same recipe. You'll create a one-of-a-kind chocolate blend, and you'll educate your palate about what impact different chocolates have on flavor.

The Tart Ring All City Bakery tarts are made in bottomless molds known as flan rings. The four-inch ring is our standard, and the recipes in this book are based on it. I prefer these rings to the more common fluted tart pan for several reasons. I love it purely as an object: As industrial equipment goes, it is beautiful and elegant. It's also very practical. At first, it poses a dilemma: How do you make a bottom for the pastry when there's no bottom to the ring? The answer, of course, is that the work surface becomes the ring's "bottom." The ring also presents a challenge: Its perfect form exposes imperfect work. If the finished tart shell is creased or the bottom edge is rounded, it is no fault of the ring. The ring makes skill matter.

Basing the recipes in a cookbook on a piece of baking equipment that most home bakers don't possess involves a degree of faith. In fact, you don't have to have flan rings to make these tarts; the recipes work with fluted tart pans, and if you're more comfortable with tart pans, go ahead. But working with the flan rings will expand your baking experience. You'll also make more beautiful tarts. If you cannot find flan rings in a store where you live, they are available through mail-order sources (see page 107). The rings are inexpensive and last forever.

And Other Useful Tools The more automated kitchen equipment becomes, the more removed people are from the real preparation of food. In the pastry kitchen, however, your hands remain your most vital tools. Mix with them, knead with them, roll, dust, flatten, squeeze, combine, pull, whip, separate, decorate, and taste with them. Pastry making begins with your hands. The closer to the process your hands are, the sounder your baking judgment will be.

As for mechanical means, however, a stand or a hand-held mixer is the single most useful piece of equipment you can possess. With either type, you can mix dough and whip cream, both of which are fundamental to making these tarts. For baking in quantity, a stand mixer with a 5-quart bowl is my first choice. A stand mixer frees your hands. It also has a paddle attachment, which is better for mixing dough than whisk-type beaters because it does not pull air into the dough while mixing. However, hand-held electric mixers are also an option, and the smaller size

9

of these units is actually better suited to the scale of most of these recipes than the stand variety. A few of the recipes call for a food processor, although a blender can be substituted, and a spice mill is occasionally useful. Beyond these, there are certain standard kitchen hand tools you will need to create these tarts. You may not own a four-inch-wide spatula now, but once you devote the time to making a perfect tart shell, bake it, and then break it because you tried moving it with a two-inch-wide spatula, you'll wish you had one.

There is a right piece of equipment for nearly everything you do while baking. I urge you to invest in this list of basics:

Measuring spoons and measuring cups You need these to measure accurately, or you're asking for trouble from the start.

Oven thermometer Ovens can lie: Your oven dial may be set at 350°F, but the actual temperature inside might be 400°F. Those 50 degrees can make a big difference, in all the wrong ways. An oven thermometer lets you double-check that you're baking at the right temperature.

Set of mixing bowls Metal bowls are preferable to plastic because they can be used for mixing, storage, *and* heating and cooking.

Knives Two basic knives will do: a 4-inch paring knife and an 8-inch chef's knife.

Saucepans The heavier the better: Don't buy cheap aluminum pans; invest in a set of stainless steel pots, or those made of a material such as Calphalon.

Rolling pin The basic choice is with handles or without (the "French" version), but you can search for a fiberglass rolling pin, which I prefer to the more common wooden pin because it feels so nice. And the fiberglass version, which does not have handles, doubles as a device with which you can pound a block of chilled dough to soften it.

Flan rings These are metal rings, available in diameters from 3 inches to 10 inches; we use 4-inch flan rings for all our tarts (see page 9).

Dough scraper This will clear your work surface of dough or excess flour with a few sweeping motions.

Pastry brush When you work with pastry dough, you need to dust it constantly with flour, but you don't want the flour to accumulate: Use a brush, either one designed specifically for pastry or a basic 4-inch-wide paintbrush, to clear excess flour from the dough and the work surface. I use brushes with black bristles so that if a bristle falls out of the brush, it's easy to spot.

Pastry docker This is an odd-looking object with a roller full of protruding nails attached to a handle. Rolling it back and forth over dough creates holes that allow steam to escape from the pastry as it bakes, preventing the dough from puffing up. In lieu of a pastry docker, you can jab a fork *repeatedly* over the dough to create the holes.

Offset spatulas Offset spatulas have angled blades, which make it easier to get underneath a fragile pastry and move it about. Buy one with a 2- by 2-inch blade for serving the tarts, and one with a 4-inch wide and 10-inch-long blade for transferring tart shells from baking sheets to cooling racks.

Whisks Different whisks speak to particular tasks. A rounded balloon whisk is designed to maximize the amount of air whipped into cream or egg whites. A piano whisk, with stronger wires, is used for combining ingredients, such as egg yolks and sugar, which require more force.

Fine-mesh strainer For straining custards and citrus creams; this can double as a flour sifter.

Ladle For pouring chocolate mousse and custards into tart shells; a 4-ounce ladle is the best size for the tarts in this book.

Sifter For sifting dry ingredients together and for dusting the tops of tarts with cocoa or confectioners' sugar.

Rubber spatulas For scraping every drop of custards and creams from bowls, for straining liquids and/or pastry creams through the strainers, and for folding ingredients together.

Insulated baking sheets These protect the bottoms of tart shells from the oven's heat. Cushionaire is one commonly available brand.

Propane gas torch This may seem a bit industrial for your kitchen, but in fact, it's simple to use and has a wide range of pastry uses, such as caramelizing the tops of tarts, browning the tips of meringue, and loosening chilled fillings from their molds. If you bake with any regularity, this should be standard equipment. Propane torches are sold in hardware stores; I recommend spending the few extra dollars to buy the kind with a trigger nozzle.

Scissors Handy for general use and, in particular, for cutting off the tip of a small paper pastry bag.

Twelve-inch ruler Takes some of the guesswork away.

Parchment paper Whether they are chilling in the freezer or are baked and waiting to be served, I set all the tarts on baking sheets lined with parchment paper. Parchment paper is also used to make small pastry bags used for design.

Eight-inch tongs Many of the fruit-filled tarts in this book are baked with the flan rings still on. Tongs make it easy to slide the hot rings off the pastry.

Miscellaneous Long-handled wooden spoons, long-handled slotted metal spoons, storage containers with tight-fitting lids, zesters, melon baller, apple corer, fruit and vegetable peeler.

Don't buy kitchen equipment that's not essential. There is a proliferation of supposed convenience gadgets for the kitchen, whose values range from dubious to worthless. Spend the money on high-quality equipment you can really use instead.

MASTER RECIPES AND TECHNIQUES

At the bakery, one of the things that distinguishes our tarts is that every one is made from scratch, start to finish, every morning. The idea is that at the end of the day they're all gone. For your use at home, you needn't be so vigilant. In fact, the dough for all of the tarts can be prepared as much as one month in advance and frozen. Setting the dough into the rings, the most time-consuming part of the process, can be done up to five days in advance, and then the rings can be frozen. The fillings are generally not time consuming and the assembly—with some practice—is a snap.

What you do want to be vigilant about is eating these tarts on the same day they're made. With some of the pastry, this is absolutely imperative. For example, once a Vanilla Bean Crème Brûlée Tart has been caramelized, it must be eaten within hours or the sugar on top will turn into a pool of syrup. For other tarts, eating them on the same day is not absolutely necessary, but they'll absolutely taste better. The integrity of the crust suffers the most, getting softer and losing its fine texture if a finished tart sits for too long. These pastries are built purely for quality, not longevity. In the rare case of leftovers, phone the neighbors.

This makes a cookielike crust, a sort of pastry cousin to the French *sablé* with its fine crumb. There are several advantages to this pastry. First is its ability to be worked often—actually kneaded like a bread dough—with no loss in the quality of its texture. Take advantage of this. Since I suggest that tarts be made in flan rings, which may be new to you, rather than fluted tart pans, use the leeway that this recipe provides, and practice again and again with the same piece of dough. Second, if you're baking a tart shell "blind"—that is, without a filling—this dough does not need to be filled with pie weights or beans to keep the sides from collapsing. After making the dough and filling the rings, just chill the dough, then put it right in the oven.

STANDARD TART DOUGH

13 tablespoons unsalted butter, cut into 13 pieces
⅓ cup confectioners' sugar
1 large egg yolk
1½ cups unbleached all-purpose flour
1 tablespoon heavy cream

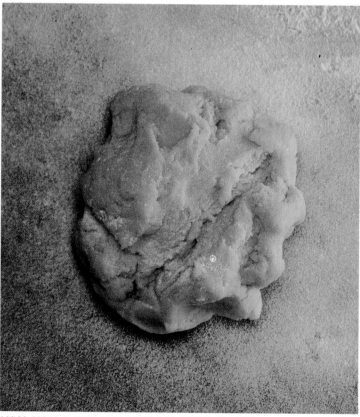

MAKES EIGHT 4-INCH TART SHELLS OR SEVEN 4¾-INCH FLUTED TART SHELLS

1) Let the butter sit at room temperature for 10 to 15 minutes. It should be malleable, but still cool.

2) Place the confectioners' sugar in the bowl of a stand mixer or a medium mixing bowl. Add the butter and toss to coat. Using the paddle attachment or a hand-held mixer, cream the sugar and butter at medium speed until the sugar is no longer visible. Scrape down the sides of the bowl. Add the egg yolk and beat until well blended. Scrape down the sides of the bowl again. Add half of the flour and beat until the dough becomes crumbly. Stop the machine, add the remaining flour and then the cream, and beat until the dough forms a sticky mass.

3) Shape the dough into a disk, and wrap well in plastic. Refrigerate until firm, approximately 2 hours.

CONTINUED

4) Dust a work surface with flour. Cut the chilled dough into 1-inch pieces. Using the heel of your hand, knead the pieces back together into a smooth disk. As you work, use a dough scraper to free the dough from the surface if necessary. Keeping the surface well dusted, roll the disk into a 12-inch log. If using flan rings, cut the log into 8 equal pieces; if using tart pans, cut into 7 pieces. Refrigerate for 5 minutes.

5) If using flan rings, line a baking sheet with parchment paper and set eight 4-inch flan rings on it.

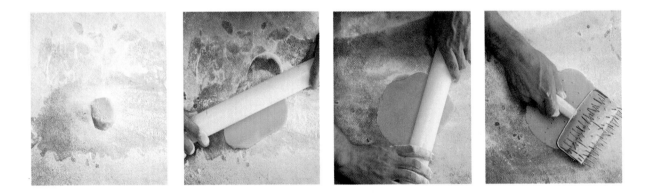

6) Dust the work surface and a rolling pin with flour. Using your fist, flatten one piece of dough into a 2- to 3-inch round. Lift it up off the work surface to dust underneath with flour. Using the rolling pin, roll the dough into a 5½-inch round, or a 6-inch round if using tart pans, about ⅛ inch thick. With a pastry docker or a fork, prick holes all over the dough. (If the dough is too soft to handle at this point, use a dough scraper to move it to a small baking sheet and refrigerate it for 2 to 3 minutes before proceeding.)

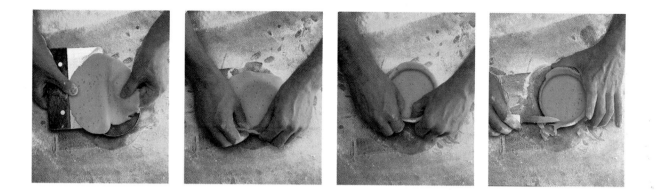

7) Center the round of dough over a flan ring or a 4¾-inch fluted tart pan with a removable bottom. If using a tart pan, be careful that the sharp top edge does not tear the dough. With your thumbs on the inside and the tips of your fingers outside, run your hands around the ring or pan several times, easing the dough down into it. Speed does not matter, finesse does. Lower your thumbs to the inside bottom of the ring and press to form a right angle between the bottom and sides of the dough. Keeping your thumbs on the inside of the ring or pan, again circle around it, applying light pressure to the sides; if you move the ring or pan around through your hands, the process will be easier. There should be at least a ½-inch rim of excess dough extending above the top edge. With a small knife, tilted upwards, trim the excess dough flush with the top of the ring. Or, if using a tart pan, simply roll the rolling pin over the top to trim the excess. Repeat this process with the remaining pieces of dough. (Refrigerate the scraps from each piece as you work, then combine them and refrigerate or freeze for another use.) If using tart pans, place them on a baking sheet.

8) Place the tart shells in the freezer for 30 minutes.

9) Position a rack in the center of the oven, and preheat the oven to 375°F.

10) If you are partially baking the tart shells, bake for 10 to 12 minutes, until the pastry is light golden brown and the interior is dry. If the bottoms of the shells puff up as they bake, tap down lightly with your fingers as often as necessary. Leave the tart shells on the baking sheet in their rings as they're easy to break and as you'll need them on the sheet in order to return them to the oven.

If you are fully baking the tart shells, bake for 12 to 15 minutes, or until golden brown. If using flan rings, remove them, and, using a wide spatula, transfer the shells to a wire rack to cool. If using tart pans, let the tart shells cool completely in the pans on a rack before unmolding them.

working notes: 1) Dusting the work surface *and* the rolling pin frequently makes rolling out the dough easy. To dust, take a large pinch of flour and throw it into the air *just above* the work surface so that it comes down in a thin, even coating. This dough can be rolled out on marble, wood, Formica, Corian—even polyurethane cutting boards if well dusted. The colder the work surface, the better. Do not roll out dough on a surface that is even slightly warm. **2)** If the dough is slippery on the inside when you are fitting it into the ring or pan, coat your fingertips in flour for better traction. If the dough tears at any point, simply patch it with the scraps. **3)** Once the dough has been laid into the ring, carefully check the bottom to see that the dough meets the ring all around the bottom edge. **4)** The tart shells will bake more evenly if you rotate the baking sheet at least once. This is especially important if you are aware that your oven has a hot spot. **5)** Those who are experienced at working with dough may get as many as ten 4-inch tart shells from this recipe. The recipe, however, is designed to provide the novice with some extra dough to work with. Also, as most of the filling recipes are for 6 shells, by baking 8 tart shells, you'll have 2 insurance shells if the sides of any of the shells should fall. (With practice, however, this should not happen.) **6)** This dough can be frozen, well wrapped in plastic, for up to 1 month. Let it thaw in the refrigerator for 1 day before working with it. The dough can be set into the rings on a sheet pan and frozen, uncovered, for up to 5 days before baking. The tart dough can go right from the freezer to the oven. Once baked, the tart shells will keep at room temperature for 2 days. Do not store baked tart shells in the refrigerator, as the moisture will affect their texture.

Variations

Hazelnut Tart Dough This pastry is as light as air, but *extremely* fragile, both before and after baking. Practice first with the Standard Tart Dough before working with this one.

Reduce the flour to 1 cup plus 2 tablespoons, and add ⅓ cup finely ground unblanched hazelnuts to the flour.

Coconut Tart Dough Unsweetened shredded coconut is available in health food stores.

Reduce the flour to 1 cup plus 2 tablespoons, and add ½ cup unsweetened shredded coconut to the flour.

Cracked Pepper Tart Dough Sounds scary, tastes great. A nice accent with fruit and honey fillings.

Add 1 teaspoon coarsely ground white or black pepper to the flour.

Candied Ginger Tart Dough This adds depth and spice to citrus cream or fruit fillings. Candied ginger is available in specialty food stores and some supermarkets.

Add 2 tablespoons finely chopped crystallized ginger to the flour.

How to Make Miniature Tarts

Follow the instructions for the Standard Tart Dough through step 3.

4) Dust a work surface with flour. Cut the chilled dough into 1-inch pieces. Using the heel of your hand, knead the pieces back together into a smooth disk. As you work, use a dough scraper to free the dough from the surface if necessary. Keeping the surface well dusted, roll the disk into a 10-inch log. Cut the pieces into 2 equal pieces and refrigerate for 5 minutes.

5) Arrange 9 miniature tart pans close together in a square (3 rows of 3, with the sides touching) on the work surface. Dust the work surface next to the tart pans with flour. Using your fist, flatten one piece of dough into a 2- to 3-inch round. Lift it up off the work surface to dust underneath with flour. Using a floured rolling pin, roll the dough into an 8-inch square.

6) Carefully lift up the dough and lay it over the the tart pans. Roll the rolling pin gently back and forth over the dough to cut the dough. With your thumbs on the inside and the tips of your fingers outside, press the dough tightly down into the bottom and up the sides of each pan. Trim away any excess dough with a small knife. Place the tart pans on a baking sheet and refrigerate the tart shells. Collect the scraps of dough and refrigerate them. Repeat the entire process with the remaining dough, then reknead and roll the scraps of dough to form more tart shells.

7) Position a rack in the center of the oven and preheat the oven to 375°F.

8) With the tip of a small knife, puncture several holes in the dough in each tart pan. Place the baking sheet in the oven and bake for 10 minutes. Turn the baking sheet around and bake for another 3 to 5 minutes, until the pastry is dry and golden brown, if using the Standard Tart Dough, or is dry and smells nicely of chocolate, if using the Chocolate Tart Dough. Let the tart shells cool in the pans on a rack, then slide each tart shell gently out of its pan.

MAKES 28-34 MINIATURE TART SHELLS

The chocolate flavor of this dough comes from cocoa powder, so the quality of cocoa you use will bear greatly on the results. Buy the best Dutch-processed cocoa powder you can find, preferably an imported brand such as Valrhona or Droste. The method used here is the same as for the Standard Tart Dough, but the baking presents an additional challenge. As the tart is a deep shade of cocoa, color won't help much to determine when it's finished. Engage your senses of smell and touch: A rich chocolate aroma and a dry interior mean the tart shells are done. If the tarts are close to being finished but you're not sure, pull them from the oven. It's fine to put them back in the oven if they do need additional time.

CHOCOLATE TART DOUGH

8 tablespoons (1 stick) unsalted butter, cut into 8 pieces

1 cup minus 2 tablespoons unbleached all-purpose flour

2 tablespoons plus 2 teaspoons unsweetened Dutch-processed cocoa powder

½ cup plus 2 tablespoons confectioners' sugar

1 large egg yolk

1) Let the butter sit at room temperature for 10 to 15 minutes. It should be malleable, but still cool.

2) Sift together the flour and cocoa powder.

3) Place the confectioners' sugar in the bowl of a stand mixer or a medium mixing bowl. Add the butter and toss to coat. Using the paddle attachment, or a hand-held mixer, cream the sugar and butter at medium speed until the sugar is no longer visible. Scrape down the sides of the bowl. Add the egg yolk and beat until well blended. Scrape down the sides of the bowl again. Add half of the flour mixture and beat until the dough becomes crumbly. Stop the machine, add the remaining flour mixture, and beat until the dough forms a sticky mass. Shape the dough into a disk and wrap well in plastic. Refrigerate until firm, approximately 2 hours.

4) Dust a work surface with flour. Cut the chilled dough into 1-inch pieces. Using the heel of your hand, knead the pieces back together into a smooth disk. As you work, use a dough scraper to free the dough from the surface if necessary. Keeping the surface well dusted, roll the disk into a 10-inch log. If using flan rings, cut the log into 7 equal pieces; if using tart pans, cut it into 6 pieces. Refrigerate for 5 minutes.

5) If using flan rings, line a baking sheet with parchment paper and set seven 4-inch flan rings on it.

MAKES SEVEN 4-INCH TART SHELLS OR
SIX 4¾-INCH FLUTED TART SHELLS

6) Dust the work surface and a rolling pin with flour. Using your fist, flatten one piece of dough into a 2- to 3-inch round. Lift it up off the work surface to dust underneath with flour. Using the rolling pin, roll the dough into a 5½-inch round, or a 6-inch round if using tart pans, about ⅛ inch thick. With a pastry docker or a fork, prick holes all over the dough. (If the dough is too soft to handle at this point, use a dough scraper to remove it to a small baking sheet and refrigerate it for 2 to 3 minutes before proceeding.)

7) Center the round of dough over a flan ring or a 4¾-inch fluted tart pan with a removable bottom. If using a tart pan, be careful that the sharp top edge does not tear the dough. With your thumbs on the inside and the tips of your fingers outside, run your hands around the ring or pan several times, easing the dough down into it. Speed does not matter, finesse does. Lower your thumbs to the inside bottom of the ring and press to form a right angle between the bottom and sides of the dough; if using a tart pan, press to form a clean angle without excess dough buildup. Keeping your thumbs on the inside of the ring or pan, again circle around it, applying light pressure to the sides; if you move the ring or pan around through your hands, the process will be easier. There should be at least a ½-inch rim of excess dough extending straight above the top edge. With a small knife, tilted upward, trim the excess dough flush with the top of the ring. Or, if using a tart pan, simply roll the rolling pin over the top to trim the excess. Repeat this process with the remaining pieces of dough. Refrigerate the scraps from each piece as you work, then knead them together and roll out another tart shell. If using tart pans, place them on a baking sheet.

8) Place the tart shells in the freezer for 30 minutes.

9) Position a rack in the center of the oven, and preheat the oven to 375°F.

10) If you are partially baking the tart shells, bake for 8 to 10 minutes, until the interiors are dry and the pastry smell nicely of chocolate. If the bottoms of the shells puff up, tap down lightly with your fingers as often as necessary. Leave the tart shells on the baking sheet in their rings or pans.

If you are fully baking the tart shells, bake for 10 to 12 minutes, until the interiors are dry and there is a deep chocolate aroma. If using flan rings, remove the rings and, using a wide spatula, transfer the shells to a wire rack to cool. If using tart pans, let the shells cool completely in the pans on a rack before unmolding.

working note: To dust the work surface and rolling pin when working with chocolate dough, sift together 2 parts flour and 1 part cocoa powder and follow notes 1 through 6 on pages 19–20.

How to Make a Paper Pastry Bag

1) Cut a piece of parchment, wax paper, or heavy bonded typing paper into a 5- by 7-inch rectangle. Cut it in half on the diagonal.

2) Hold the triangle midway on the long side (with your left hand if you're right-handed). With your right hand, twist the bottom point in on itself to form a cone. Leave a generous opening (at least 1½ inches wide). Pull the point up to tighten and to form a sharp tip.

3) Grasping the newly formed cone in your right hand at the open end, twist the tail around the cone, pulling it up toward you to tighten.

4) Fold the ends inside the cone to secure.

Melting Chocolate Bittersweet chocolate is used to draw different designs and to write on many of these tarts.

There are several ways to melt a small quantity of chocolate: Begin by placing finely chopped chocolate in a small bowl, preferably metal if not using a microwave.

Option 1: Place the bowl above a pilot light on top of the stove. Let sit until melted, 20 to 30 minutes. (This will take less time if the oven is on.) Stir occasionally.

Option 2: Place 1 inch of water in a medium saucepan and bring to a simmer. Remove from the heat, and float the bowl of chocolate on the water until the chocolate is melted. Pay special care that not a single drop of water enters the bowl of chocolate.

Option 3: Place the bowl of chocolate in a microwave oven, and follow the manufacturer's instructions.

Filling the Bag

1) Holding the pastry bag in your left hand (if right-handed), spoon in the melted chocolate until half full. (It's important that it's not more than half full.)

2) Using little crimps and folds, tightly fold the bag down to meet the chocolate. Snip off the slightest bit from the point. (It shouldn't be much larger than a pencil point.)

Drawing Lines and Dots For lines: The trick with drawing lines is speed. Get your line started before it reaches the tart. Have enough workspace around the tart. The quickest flick of your wrist and forearm, started as much as 12 inches before the tart, and ending a bit after it, should assure a perfect line. From start to finish apply pressure to the chocolate to keep it flowing.

For dots: Put the tip of the bag up to the surface without touching it and squeeze until a small dot comes out. Halfway into the dot, stop squeezing and lift the bag up and away. A dot will set in a few seconds.

Summer Fruit Tart with Lemon Cream

Tapioca Custard with Sweet or Sour Cherries

Champagne Peach Tart with Vanilla Sugar

Chocolate Custard Infused with Ethiopian Coffee Beans

Plums Baked in Toasted Almond Cream

Blueberry-Coconut Tart

Ricotta Cheese Tart with Summer Fruits and Flowers

Earl Grey Tea Pastry Cream in a Chocolate Tart Shell

World's First Stuffed Raspberry Tart™

Maple Whipped Cream Tart with a Side of Maple-Baked Walnuts

Lime Cream in a Candied Ginger Crust

Shaved Honeydew with Blackberries

Tart Dough Cookies, Three or Four Raspberries, and a Glass of Bonny Doon Wine

Mini Strawberry–White Chocolate Tart

Sake-Spiked Plum Tart with Ginger

Cherries on Two-Tone Chocolate

Sautéed Apricots on Thyme-Honey Whipped Cream

Zinfandel-Marinated Cherries with Cocoa

Muskmelon in a Geometric State of Mind

Chocolate Mousse with a Blackberry Blend

THE TARTS OF SPRING AND SUMMER

Springtime is when the Greenmarket comes alive. Strawberries arrive in May, the first in a procession of fruits that includes sugar plums, gooseberries, red currants, and tiny wild blueberries. Standards like blueberries, peaches, and apricots are in abundance. Cherries come to market both sweet and sour. The only fruit that I've ever been disappointed in at the market is white peaches, which have never tasted as wonderful as the ones I've had in France. *C'est la vie.* I'm lucky enough to be working with some of the best raw materials that any bakery could hope for.

The only negative to all of this is that New Yorkers go out of town in droves during the hot weather. It seems as if while we're in the kitchen making some of the nicest tarts of the year, all of Manhattan is away at the beach. A lot of our regular customers never even see or taste how good the tarts of spring and summer get—maybe now they'll make them themselves.

The fruits that we use for this tart rotate throughout the summer. They include red, black, and gold raspberries, wild blueberries, strawberries, melons, figs, peaches, gooseberries, and red currants. Only the figs are not grown locally, but I like them too much to leave them out. Fruit tart aficionados, please note: There's absolutely no reason to shellac the top of fruit tarts with that ubiquitous layer of apricot glaze. It looks amateurish and has nothing to do with good taste. Let the beauty and flavor of fresh fruit stand on their own.

SUMMER FRUIT TART WITH LEMON CREAM

1 cup granulated sugar	
Grated zest of 1 lemon (see step 1)	
½ cup freshly squeezed lemon juice	
4 large eggs	
1 large egg yolk	
12 tablespoons unsalted butter, cut into 12 pieces	
12 fully baked tart shells, made with Standard Tart Dough (page 16)	
2 cups cut-up assorted seasonal fruits and/or whole berries	

1) Place the sugar in a medium bowl and grate the zest of 1 lemon into it. Rub the sugar and zest together between the palms of your hands.

2) Pour the juice into a medium nonreactive saucepan. Add the eggs, egg yolk, butter, and the zested sugar, and whisk to combine. Set the pan over medium heat and cook, whisking constantly, for 3 to 5 minutes, until the mixture begins to thicken. Be sure to whisk all over the bottom of the pan, especially the edges. At the first sign of a boil, remove from the heat and strain through a sieve into a bowl.

3) With a ladle or a large spoon, fill each tart shell nearly to the top with the lemon cream. Refrigerate for 20 to 25 minutes or until set.

4) Arrange the fruit in free-form patterns on the tops of the tarts, and serve.

MAKES 6 TARTS

True to the tapioca pudding my mother made when I was young, I more or less took the recipe printed on a box of Minute Tapioca and adjusted it to my taste. Needless to say, the box doesn't call for fresh cherries or a vanilla bean, but they're a nice touch.

TAPIOCA CUSTARD WITH SWEET OR SOUR CHERRIES

1 cup milk
½ vanilla bean, split
⅓ cup Minute Tapioca
½ cup granulated sugar
1 large egg yolk
½ cup heavy cream
½ pint sweet or sour cherries, pitted and coarsely chopped, plus 6 cherries with stems intact, for garnish
6 fully baked tart shells made with Standard Tart Dough (page 16)

1) Pour the milk into a medium saucepan. Scrape the seeds from the vanilla bean into the milk, along with the bean. Add the tapioca and sugar, and whisk to combine. Set the pan over medium heat and whisk gently until the milk comes to a simmer. Remove from the heat and set aside for 3 to 5 minutes to allow the tapioca to thicken.

2) Place the egg yolk in a medium bowl, and add half of the tapioca mixture, whisking until well blended. Return the mixture to the saucepan, set over medium heat, and bring just to a boil, whisking constantly. Remove from the heat, and immediately pour into a medium bowl. Whisk in the cream. Refrigerate for 30 minutes, until cool, whisking every 5 minutes.

3) Spread the chopped cherries in the bottom of the tart shells. Using a ladle or a large spoon, fill the tart shells with the tapioca custard. Refrigerate for 30 minutes.

4) Place a cherry in the center of each tart, and serve.

MAKES 6 TARTS

On the one hand, you don't need to buy expensive Champagne for this recipe, because it gets heated, changing its taste. On the other hand, you may *want* to buy expensive Champagne, because half of the bottle is left over to serve with the tarts. You choose.

CHAMPAGNE PEACH TART WITH VANILLA SUGAR

2 cups Champagne

1 vanilla bean, split

2 tablespoons granulated sugar

3 large ripe peaches, pitted and cut into 12 slices each

6 partially baked tarts shells (see note), made with Standard Tart Dough (page 16), rings left on

3 tablespoons unsalted butter, cut into small cubes

1 tablespoon Vanilla Sugar (see note)

1) Pour the Champagne into a medium saucepan. Scrape the seeds from the vanilla bean into the Champagne, then add the bean. Add the sugar, set the pan over medium heat, and heat, stirring, just until the sugar has dissolved. Remove from the heat and let cool to lukewarm.

2) Add the peaches to the Champagne mixture, and macerate for at least 30 minutes, or up to 1 hour, at room temperature.

3) Preheat the oven to 375°F.

4) Using a slotted spoon, transfer the peaches to a bowl. Arrange 6 peach slices in each tart shell, placing 3 slices around the sides and stacking 3 slices in the middle. Spoon 3 tablespoons of the Champagne mixture over the peaches in each tart, then dot with the butter. Sprinkle half of the Vanilla Sugar on top of the tarts.

5) Bake for 20 to 25 minutes, until the juices are bubbling slowly around the edges of the tarts. Remove from the oven and let sit for 30 seconds, then remove the rings with a pair of tongs. Using a wide spatula, transfer to a wire rack. Sprinkle with the remaining Vanilla Sugar, and let cool for 30 minutes. Serve with Champagne.

ingredient note: To make Vanilla Sugar, place ½ cup granulated sugar in a medium bowl. Split 4 vanilla beans and, with a small paring knife, scrape the seeds into the sugar. Reserve the beans. Rub the sugar and vanilla seeds between your fingertips to disperse the seeds throughout the sugar. Sift the vanilla sugar into a container. Cut the vanilla beans into pieces, and add them to the vanilla sugar. Cover tightly and store at room temperature.

working note: If using tart pans, leave the partially baked shells in the pans. Cool the baked tarts in the pans on a wire rack for 30 minutes, then unmold.

MAKES 6 TARTS

Why Ethiopian? Because coffee beans from that country taste like chocolate. Combining these particular beans with dark chocolate creates an unusually deep chocolate-coffee flavor. Specialty food stores and coffee bars should carry Ethiopian coffee beans. If you can't find them, try Kenyan AA, which has similar characteristics.

CHOCOLATE CUSTARD INFUSED WITH ETHIOPIAN COFFEE BEANS

3 large egg yolks

1½ cups heavy cream

1 heaping tablespoon coarsely ground Ethiopian coffee beans

3½ ounces bittersweet chocolate, finely chopped

6 fully baked tart shells, made with Chocolate Tart Dough (page 22)

1 ounce bittersweet chocolate, melted, for design

1) Place the egg yolks in a medium bowl.

2) Pour the heavy cream into a small saucepan and bring to a simmer. Remove from the heat and add the coffee beans. Let infuse for exactly 1 minute, whisking several times. Strain the cream through a fine sieve into a medium saucepan.

3) Bring the coffee cream to a simmer. Remove from the heat, add the chocolate, and let sit for 1 minute. Whisk until smooth. Slowly add the cream to the egg yolks, whisking constantly. Strain into a bowl.

4) With a ladle or a large spoon, fill the tart shells with the chocolate custard. Refrigerate for at least 30 minutes, or until set.

5) Fill a small paper pastry bag (see page 24) with the melted chocolate. Stripe and dot the top of each tart to make a simple design. Let sit at room temperature for 10 minutes before serving.

MAKES 6 TARTS

In the middle of the summer, when everyone at the Greenmarket is busy buying up the raspberries, blueberries, and peaches, I turn to the small, almost-secret collection of plums. Some of the varieties, like Burbank, Shiro, and New Jersey sugar plums, last only a week or two on the stands. You may not find those varieties, but Santa Rosa plums are widely available and make a perfect tart.

PLUMS BAKED IN TOASTED ALMOND CREAM

3 ounces (a scant cup) slivered almonds

¾ cup confectioners' sugar

6 tablespoons unsalted butter, cut into 6 pieces and slightly softened

1 large egg yolk

6 partially baked tart shells (see note), made with Standard Tart Dough (page 16) or Candied Ginger Tart Dough (page 20), rings left on

7 small to medium Santa Rosa plums, pitted and cut into 6 slices each

1) Preheat the oven to 375°F.

2) Spread the almonds on a baking sheet, and toast in the oven until golden brown, approximately 5 minutes. Let cool, then transfer to a food processor or nut grinder and process or grind until coarsely ground. Set aside.

3) Place the confectioners' sugar in the bowl of a stand mixer or a medium mixing bowl. Add the butter and toss to coat. Using the paddle attachment or a hand-held mixer, beat at medium speed until the confectioners' sugar has disappeared. Add the almonds, beat for 30 seconds, then add the egg yolk and beat until blended.

4) Divide the almond mixture among the tarts shells, spreading it evenly over the bottoms. Stand 3 plum slices on end in a row down the center of each tart. Stand 2 more slices on either side of each row.

5) Bake for 25 to 30 minutes, until the almond cream is puffed and golden brown around the edges but still light and soft in the center. The plum slices will settle into the tarts as they bake and the tips may be slightly blackened. Remove from the oven and let sit for 30 seconds, then remove the rings with tongs. Using a wide spatula, transfer to a wire rack and let cool.

working note: If using tart pans, leave the partially baked shells in the pans. Cool the baked tarts in the pans on a wire rack, then unmold.

serving note: I like these tarts best completely cooled, but a strong case can be made to serve them warm from the oven, with vanilla or caramel ice cream on the side.

MAKES 6 TARTS

before

after

way after

I'm not the outdoors type—mountains and lakes are nice, but I prefer the streets of New York City. Even so, my instinct tells me that this is the ideal tart for a picnic: It's easy and quick to make, and it's sturdy, so it travels well.

BLUEBERRY-COCONUT TART

¾ cup granulated sugar

¾ cup plus 2 tablespoons heavy cream

1 pint blueberries

1¼ cups unsweetened shredded coconut

6 partially baked tart shells (see note), made with Standard Tart Dough (page 16), rings left on

1) Preheat the oven to 350°F.

2) Combine the sugar and cream in a small saucepan and heat over medium heat, stirring gently, until the sugar has dissolved. Remove from the heat and let cool for 10 minutes.

3) Combine the blueberries and coconut in a medium bowl. Add the cream mixture, and stir to mix well.

4) Place the tart shells on a baking sheet lined with parchment paper. Divide the blueberry mixture evenly among the tart shells, mounding the blueberries and coconut in the center of the shells.

5) Bake for 20 to 25 minutes, until the coconut is lightly toasted and the juices are bubbling around the edges. Remove from the oven and let sit for 30 seconds, then remove the rings with tongs. Using a wide spatula, transfer to a wire rack, and let cool for 30 minutes.

working note: If using tart pans, leave the partially baked shells in the pans. Cool the baked tarts in the pans on a wire rack for 30 minutes, then unmold.

MAKES 6 TARTS

Easiest tart in the book. The hardest part may be finding freshly made ricotta cheese. Well-made ricotta is like the first step that milk takes on the path to becoming cheese. It's soft and creamy, and its taste personifies fresh. If you live in or near a city with an Italian community, check the grocery stores in those neighborhoods. If not, try to convince your favorite specialty store or cheese shop to carry it.

RICOTTA CHEESE TART WITH SUMMER FRUITS AND FLOWERS

2 cups fresh ricotta cheese

2 tablespoons honey

2 tablespoons heavy cream

1½ cups blueberries, raspberries, and/or gooseberries

6 fully baked tart shells, made with Standard Tart Dough (page 16) or Cracked Pepper Tart Dough (page 20)

12 to 18 edible flowers

1 teaspoon Vanilla Sugar (see page 32), optional

1) Combine the ricotta cheese, honey, and heavy cream in a medium bowl. With a large spoon or spatula, gently blend the ingredients. Fold in half of the fruit.

2) Spoon the ricotta mixture into the tart shells. Arrange the remaining fruit and the flowers on top, and sprinkle with the Vanilla Sugar if desired.

working note: The moisture in fresh ricotta cheese will weaken the texture of the tart shells after 2 to 3 hours. Since the assembly of this tart takes practically no time, prepare it as close to serving time as possible.

MAKES 6 TARTS

A friend who is a chocolate maker in Chicago sent a box of chocolates to me at the bakery. I tasted a few, then packed up the box to take home with some papers. When I got to my door, I could here the phone ringing inside. I rushed in, threw down everything I was holding, and ran for the phone. Later that night, as I was getting into bed it hit me: I had thrown the chocolates onto the stove. I rushed downstairs and confirmed the worst: Bull's-eye on the pilot light. In the box, which had become chocolate soup, there was one survivor. One heroic chocolate, which somehow, had not melted. I took it, held it up, thanked it, and ate it. It had an Earl Grey tea filling.

EARL GREY TEA PASTRY CREAM IN A CHOCOLATE TART SHELL

2½ cups milk
6 Earl Grey teabags
4 large egg yolks
⅔ cup granulated sugar
2 tablespoons unbleached all-purpose flour
1 tablespoon cornstarch
1 tablespoon plus 1 teaspoon apricot preserves
6 fully baked tart shells, made with Chocolate Tart Dough (page 22)
1 ounce bittersweet chocolate, melted, for design

1) Pour the milk into a small saucepan and bring to a simmer over medium heat. Cut open the tea bags, empty the loose tea leaves into the milk, and remove from the heat. Let cool completely, then strain the milk through a fine sieve into a medium saucepan.

2) Place the egg yolks in a medium bowl, add the sugar, and whisk to combine. Whisk in the flour and cornstarch.

3) Bring the milk back to a simmer. Pour half of it into the egg yolk mixture, whisking constantly until smooth. Then pour the mixture back into the saucepan. Cook over medium heat, whisking, until the mixture thickens and comes to a boil. Boil for 5 seconds, then whisk once more forcefully around the pan, and transfer to a medium bowl. Place plastic wrap directly on the surface of the pastry cream and puncture several holes in it with a paring knife. Refrigerate until cool.

4) Spread the apricot preserves evenly over the bottoms of the tart shells. Whisk the pastry cream until it is smooth, and spoon it into the tart shells. Refrigerate for 15 minutes.

5) Fill a small paper pastry bag (see page 24) with the melted chocolate. Stripe and dot the top of each tart.

MAKES 6 TARTS

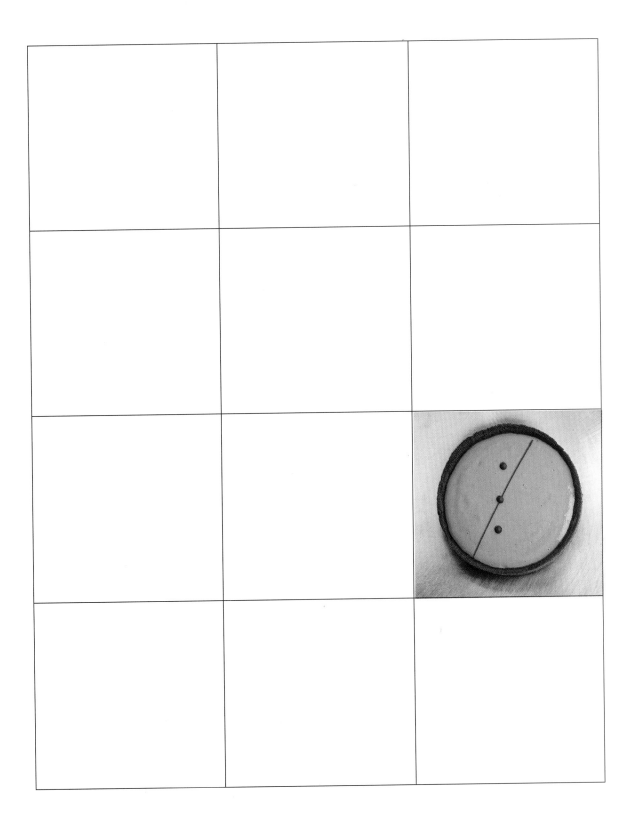

To me, the hollow interior of the raspberry calls out for a filling. Customers are always excited when they realize that what's stuffed is the raspberry itself! Form and function.

WORLD'S FIRST STUFFED RASPBERRY TART™

2 ounces bittersweet chocolate, melted

1 pint raspberries

1½ cups heavy cream

1 tablespoon Vanilla Sugar (see page 32) or granulated sugar

6 fully baked tart shells, made with Chocolate Tart Dough (page 22)

1) Line a baking sheet with parchment paper.

2) Fill two or three small paper pastry bags (see page 24) with the melted chocolate. Cut a small opening in the tip of one, and set the others aside in a warm place.

3) To stuff the raspberries, hold each berry upside down and pipe chocolate into the interior, then lay the berry on its side on the prepared baking sheet. Refrigerate for 15 minutes.

4) Pour the cream into the bowl of a stand mixer or a medium mixing bowl. Using the whisk attachment or a hand-held mixer, beat at medium speed until soft peaks form. Beat in the sugar. Spoon the whipped cream into the tart shells. Refrigerate for 15 minutes.

5) Mound the raspberries into small pyramids in the centers of the tarts, leaving a border of cream around them, and serve.

MAKES 6 TARTS

Making maple syrup can be brutal work, as I found out when I spent a week in the Vermont woods with maple syrup makers Howie and Stephan Cantor. With only a few people, tapping holes in sixty acres of maple trees is hard enough. Then the sap starts running, and the work goes round the clock for days, feeding logs to a fire and boiling the sap down. Fortunately, compared to the labor involved in making the syrup, making this tart is a breeze.

MAPLE WHIPPED CREAM TART WITH A SIDE OF MAPLE-BAKED WALNUTS

About ¼ teaspoon canola oil or vegetable oil

1½ cups (6 ounces) walnut halves or pieces

¾ cup best-quality pure maple syrup

1 cup heavy cream

6 fully baked tart shells, made with Standard Tart Dough (page 16)

1) Preheat the oven to 375°F. Line a small baking sheet with parchment paper or aluminum foil and grease with the oil.

2) Put the walnuts in a medium baking dish, add ½ cup of the maple syrup, and toss to coat. Bake for 15 minutes, or until the syrup has baked onto the nuts. Spread the walnuts on the prepared baking sheet. If there are any large clusters of nuts, separate them. Let cool.

3) Pour the cream into the bowl of a stand mixer or a mixing bowl. Using the whisk attachment, or a hand-held mixer, beat the cream at medium speed until soft peaks form. Add the remaining ¼ cup maple syrup and beat for a few more seconds, just to blend.

4) Spoon the maple whipped cream into the tart shells. Serve the walnuts on the side, in individual ramekins or on the same plates as the tarts.

MAKES 6 TARTS

Of all the bowls in our kitchen, if I could lick just one, it would be the bowl with the lime cream in it.

LIME CREAM IN A CANDIED GINGER CRUST

	1 cup granulated sugar
	Grated zest of 1 lime (see step1)
	1/2 cup freshly squeezed lime juice (3 to 4 limes)
	4 large eggs
	1 large egg yolk
	6 tablespoons unsalted butter, cut into 6 pieces
	6 fully baked tart shells, made with Candied Ginger Tart Dough (page 20)

1) Place the sugar in a medium bowl and zest the lime into it. Rub the zest and sugar together between the palms of your hands.

2) Combine the lime juice, eggs, egg yolk, butter, and the zested sugar in a medium nonreactive saucepan, and whisk to blend. Set the pan over medium heat and cook, whisking constantly for 3 to 5 minutes, until the mixture begins to thicken. Be sure to whisk all over the bottom of the pan, especially the edges. At the first sign of a boil, remove from the heat and strain through a sieve into a bowl.

3) With a ladle or a large spoon, fill the tart shells with the lime cream. Refrigerate for 30 minutes, or until set.

4) Let sit at room temperature for 10 minutes before serving.

MAKES 6 TARTS

The shaved honeydew is the result of using a vegetable peeler to render paper-thin slices of the fruit. This is one of those tarts that causes people to say silly things like, "My God, it's too pretty to eat!" For my taste, nothing is too pretty to eat.

SHAVED HONEYDEW WITH BLACKBERRIES

1 cup granulated sugar
Grated zest of 1 lime (see step 1)
Grated zest of ½ lemon (see step 1)
½ cup freshly squeezed lemon and lime juice (2 lemons and 2 limes)
4 large eggs
1 large egg yolk
6 tablespoons unsalted butter, cut into 6 pieces
6 fully baked tart shells, made with Standard Tart Dough (page 16)
¼ honeydew melon
18 blackberries
12 to 18 edible flowers (see note)

1) Place the sugar in a medium bowl and zest the lime and lemon into it. Rub the zests and sugar together between the palms of your hands.

2) Strain the citrus juice into a medium nonreactive saucepan. Add the eggs, egg yolk, butter, and the zested sugar, and whisk to combine. Set the pan over medium heat and cook, whisking constantly, for 3 to 5 minutes, until the mixture begins to thicken. Be sure to whisk all over the bottom of the pan, especially the edges. At the first sign of a boil, remove from the heat and strain through a sieve into a bowl.

3) With a ladle or a large spoon, fill the tart shells with the citrus cream. Refrigerate for 15 to 20 minutes, until set.

4) Using a vegetable peeler, shave paper-thin slices approximately 2 inches long and 1 inch wide from the melon.

5) Place the tarts on individual plates, and arrange 3 or 4 melon shavings around each one in layers. Add 3 blackberries and 2 or 3 flowers on each tart, and serve.

working note: Edible flowers are extremely perishable. Keep them refrigerated until you are ready to use them.

MAKES 6 TARTS

back view ⟶

A small piece of pastry, a perfect piece of fruit, and a glass of dessert wine is a perfect dessert. This series of combinations is for Randall Grahm, who makes my favorite dessert wines at his Bonny Doon Vineyards in Santa Cruz, California.

TART DOUGH COOKIES, THREE OR FOUR RASPBERRIES, AND A GLASS OF BONNY DOON WINE

Option 1

Bonny Doon Muscat Canelli

Coconut Tart Dough (page 20)

3 or 4 raspberries per person

Option 2

Bonny Doon Gewürztraminer

Cracked Pepper Tart Dough (page 20)

2 or 3 slices of a white peach per person

Option 3

Bonny Doon Riesling

Hazelnut Tart Dough (page 20)

1 small slice of cantaloupe per person

1) Chill the wine.

2) Preheat the oven to 350°F. Line a baking sheet with parchment paper.

3) Roll the dough out to approximately ⅛ inch thick (how much dough you use depends on how many people you are serving). With a 1½-inch round cookie cutter, stamp out a few cookies for each person. Place them about 1 inch apart on the prepared baking sheet. Bake for 10 to 12 minutes, until lightly browned. Transfer to a wire rack and let cool.

4) Arrange the cookies and fruit on small plates. Pour the wine, and serve.

serving note: These wines are available only in half-sized bottles. They will serve two people comfortably, and may frustrate three.

Strawberries and cream, turned into finger food. Make these for a summer party.

MINI STRAWBERRY-WHITE CHOCOLATE TART

4 ounces white chocolate, finely chopped
1¼ cups heavy cream
30 strawberries, locally grown, if possible
24 fully baked 2½-inch tart shells, made with Chocolate Tart Dough (page 22) or Standard Tart Dough (page 16)
1 ounce bittersweet chocolate, melted, for design

1) Place the white chocolate in a medium bowl. Pour 1 cup of the cream into a saucepan and bring to a boil. Pour the hot cream all at once on top of the chocolate. Let sit for 1 minute, then whisk until smooth. Strain into a bowl. Cover the bowl with plastic wrap and puncture several holes in it with the tip of a paring knife. Refrigerate for at least 4 hours, or overnight.

2) Coarsely chop 6 of the strawberries. Divide them among the tart shells.

3) Pour the chilled white chocolate cream into the bowl of a stand mixer or a medium mixing bowl, and add the remaining ¼ cup cream. Using the whisk attachment or a hand-held mixer, beat at medium speed just until soft peaks begin to form.

4) Carefully spoon the white chocolate cream into the tart shells. Refrigerate for 15 minutes, or until set.

5) Place a whole strawberry, with its cap still on, upright on each tart. Fill a paper pastry bag (see page 24) with the melted chocolate. Pipe a single chocolate dot on the white chocolate in front of each strawberry, and serve.

MAKES 24 MINI-TARTS

Japanese food has many virtues, but dessert is not one of them. This tart borrows components from the cuisine itself: sake, a strong alcoholic drink made of fermented rice and served warm; plums, which are used to make pungent plum paste; and ginger, used in many ways but most commonly as a garnish for sushi.

SAKE-SPIKED PLUM TART WITH GINGER

2½ cups sake	
6 medium red plums, pitted and cut into 6 slices each	
4 ounces ginger, peeled and cut into 1-inch pieces	
¼ cup plus 2 tablespoons granulated sugar	
¼ cup heavy cream	
6 partially baked tart shells (see note), made with Candied Ginger Tart Dough (page 20) or Standard Tart Dough (page 16), rings left on	

1) Combine the sake, plums, ginger, and 3 tablespoons of the sugar, in a large nonreactive saucepan and heat until a few bubbles appear around the edges, just below a simmer. Remove from the heat and let sit for at least 30 minutes.

2) Preheat the oven to 375°F.

3) With a slotted spoon, transfer the plums to a medium bowl. Let cool completely. Reserve ¼ of the sake mixture.

4) Combine the remaining 3 tablespoons sugar, the cream, and the reserved sake mixture in a small saucepan, and heat, stirring gently, until the sugar has dissolved. Add half of the cream mixture to the plums, and toss to coat.

5) Place 6 plum slices in each tart shell, skin side up, arranging the fruit differently in each shell. Pour the remaining cream mixture over the plums.

6) Bake the tarts for 20 to 25 minutes, until the juices are bubbling slowly around the edges. Let sit for 30 seconds, then remove the rings with tongs. Using a wide spatula, transfer to a wire rack, and let cool for at least 20 minutes before serving.

working note: If using tart pans, leave the partially baked shells in the pans. Cool the baked tarts in the pans on a wire rack for at least 20 minutes, then unmold.

MAKES 6 TARTS

Keeping the stems on the cherries lets you pull the cherries out of the tart one by one, predipped in the "two-tone" chocolate—translated, white chocolate and dark chocolate cream side by side.

CHERRIES ON TWO-TONE CHOCOLATE

2 ounces white chocolate,
finely chopped

¾ cup plus ⅔ cup heavy cream

1½ ounces bittersweet chocolate,
finely chopped

18 dark cherries,
pitted and coarsely chopped

6 fully baked tart shells, made
with Chocolate Tart Pastry (page 22)

30 dark cherries with stems intact

1 ounce bittersweet chocolate,
melted, for design, optional

1) Place the white chocolate in a medium bowl. Pour ¾ cup of the cream into a small saucepan and bring to a boil over medium heat. Pour the hot cream all at once on top of the white chocolate. Let sit for 1 minute, then whisk until smooth. Strain into a small bowl, cover with plastic wrap, and puncture several holes in it with the tip of a paring knife. Refrigerate for at least 4 hours, or overnight. Repeat the same procedure with the bittersweet chocolate and the remaining ⅔ cup cream, and refrigerate for at least 4 hours, or overnight.

2) Divide the chopped cherries evenly among the tarts, spreading them on the bottom of each tart.

3) Scrape the chilled white chocolate cream into a mixing bowl. Using a hand-held mixer, beat at medium speed until medium peaks form. Spoon the white chocolate cream into one half of each tart shell. Beat the bittersweet chocolate cream, and fill the other halves of the shells. Gently shake the tarts to level the tops. Refrigerate for 15 minutes, or until set.

4) Arrange 5 cherries on each tart. If desired, fill a small paper pastry bag (see page 24) with the melted chocolate, and place a single dot on each tart. Serve.

MAKES 6 TARTS

If you whip cream and add honey to it, you get honey-flavored whipped cream. But if you dissolve honey in cream over heat, chill it, and then whip it, the result is a smooth, far more luscious texture. Any honey will work, but the thyme variety is especially tasty with apricots and vanilla.

SAUTÉED APRICOTS ON THYME-HONEY WHIPPED CREAM

apricot

1 cup heavy cream
½ cup honey, preferably thyme
1 tablespoon unsalted butter
5 apricots, pitted and cut into 6 slices each
1 tablespoon Vanilla Sugar (see page 32) or granulated sugar
6 fully baked tart shells, made with Standard Tart Dough (page 16)

1) Combine the cream and honey in a small saucepan and heat over medium heat, stirring, until the honey has dissolved. Transfer to a bowl, cover with plastic wrap, and puncture several holes in it with the tip of a paring knife. Refrigerate for at least 4 hours, or overnight.

2) Melt the butter in a skillet over medium heat. When the butter sizzles, add the apricots and sauté for 30 seconds. Sprinkle the sugar over the apricots and sauté for 1 minute longer, or until the fruit is heated through. Transfer to a plate and let cool.

3) Place the chilled honey cream in the bowl of a stand mixer or a mixing bowl. Using the whisk attachment or a hand-held mixer, beat at medium speed until firm but not stiff peaks form. Spoon the cream into the tart shells. Arrange 5 apricot slices in a different pattern on top of each tart, and serve.

MAKES 6 TARTS

When this dish comes out of the oven, it looks striking. As it cools, the cherries begin to wrinkle, showing the effects of the oven's heat, but if you can live with the wrinkles, this tart will amply reward you. These are elegant, sophisticated flavors. (Please note: The Zinfandel *must* be red, not white or blush.)

ZINFANDEL-MARINATED CHERRIES WITH COCOA

2 pints dark cherries, pitted
2 cups red Zinfandel
6 partially baked tart shells (see note), made with Chocolate Tart Dough (page 22), rings left on
3 tablespoons heavy cream
2 teaspoons granulated sugar
Cocoa powder, for dusting

1) Place the cherries in a medium bowl and pour the wine over them. Cover with plastic wrap and let marinate for 1 hour.

2) Preheat the oven to 350°F.

3) With a slotted spoon, transfer the cherries to a plate. Then pack them tightly into the tart shells with their smooth sides up.

4) Pour ½ cup of the Zinfandel marinade into a small nonreactive saucepan, and stir in the cream and sugar. (You won't need the rest of the marinade.) Heat, stirring, until the sugar dissolves. Remove from the heat.

5) Divide the Zinfandel cream among the tart shells. Bake for 20 to 25 minutes, until the juices are bubbling around the edges. Remove from the oven and let sit for 1 minute, then remove the rings with tongs. Using a wide spatula, transfer to a wire rack to cool.

6) Very lightly dust the tops of the tarts with cocoa powder, and serve.

working notes: 1) Sometimes the Zinfandel cream bubbles over the edges of the tart shells. It may be necessary to run a paring knife between the rings and the tart shells before removing the rings. **2)** If using tart pans, leave the partially baked shells in the pans. Cool the baked tarts in the pans on a wire rack, then unmold.

MAKES 6 TARTS

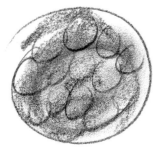

Muskmelon is like cantaloupe, and it's great with the lime cream in this tart. As for getting the melon into that "geometric state of mind," it's easy. Use an apple corer to create a perfect column of melon, cut triangles from the flesh, scoop out circles. Then arrange the fruit on the tarts in random sculptural form. There is no right or wrong way, only what's pleasing to your eye.

MUSKMELON IN A GEOMETRIC STATE OF MIND

⅔ cup granulated sugar

Grated zest of 3 limes (see step 1)

Grated zest of 1 lemon (see step 1)

½ cup lime juice (about 5 limes)

4 large eggs

1 large egg yolk

6 tablespoons unsalted butter, cut into 6 pieces

6 fully baked tart shells, made with Standard Tart Dough (page 16) or Cracked Pepper Tart Dough (page 20)

½ small muskmelon or cantaloupe, seeds removed

½ small honeydew melon

1) Place the sugar in a medium bowl, and grate the zest of the limes and lemon into it. Rub the zest and sugar together between the palms of your hands.

2) Combine the lime juice, eggs, egg yolk, butter, and the zested sugar in a medium nonreactive saucepan, and whisk to blend. Set the pan over medium heat and cook, whisking constantly, for 3 to 5 minutes, until the mixture begins to thicken. Be sure to whisk all over the bottom of the pan, especially the edges. At the first sign of a boil, remove from the heat and strain through a sieve into a bowl.

3) With a ladle or a large spoon, fill the tart shells with the lime cream. Refrigerate for 30 minutes, or until set.

4) Meanwhile, with a paring knife, melon baller, apple corer, and any other implement you can think of, cut from the melons an assortment of squares, circles, triangles, and columns about ¾ to 1 inch in size. You will need 6 to 8 pieces for each tart (36 to 48 pieces in all).

5) Arrange the fruit in a different pattern on each of the tarts: Stand the triangles point up, lean squares against circles—use your imagination. Serve.

MAKES 6 TARTS

Chocolate mousse fills most of this tart, but underneath it, there's a layer of chocolate and blackberries blended together. If you prefer raspberries to blackberries, they work well too.

CHOCOLATE MOUSSE WITH A BLACKBERRY BLEND

4 ounces bittersweet chocolate, finely chopped

⅓ cup milk

⅓ cup plus 2 tablespoons heavy cream

½ cup blackberries plus 6 perfect blackberries, for design

6 fully baked tart shells, made with Chocolate Tart Pastry (page 22)

Cocoa powder, for dusting

1) Place the chocolate in a medium bowl.

2) Combine the milk and 2 tablespoons of the cream in a saucepan, and bring just to a boil. Pour the hot milk all at once over the chocolate. Let sit for 1 minute, then whisk until smooth. Let cool to room temperature.

3) To make the blackberry blend, transfer ¼ cup of the chocolate cream to a food processor or blender. Add the ½ cup berries, and process for 15 seconds. Spoon the mixture into the centers of the tart shells, spreading it into a 2-inch circle in each one.

4) Pour the remaining ⅓ cup cream into a mixing bowl. Using a hand-held mixer, beat at medium speed just until soft peaks form. Fold the whipped cream into the cooled chocolate cream.

5) Spoon or ladle the chocolate mousse into the tart shells. Refrigerate for 30 minutes, or until set.

6) Dust the tarts lightly with cocoa powder, and place a berry on top of each one. Let sit at room temperature for 10 minutes before serving.

MAKES 6 TARTS

Orange Tart Made out of Apples

Lemon Tart, Four Ways

Lemon Meringue Tart, Manhattan Style

Tropical Chocolate Tart

Square Pear Peg Tart

Milky Way Tart

Banana Chocolate Chunk Tart

Chocolate Mousse Tart

Passion Fruit Tart with a Raspberry Polka Dot

Grapes Baked with Hazelnuts

White Chocolate Infused with Pear Skins

Pear, Pineapple, and Pepper

Mint Chocolate Chip Tart

Vanilla Bean Crème Brûlée Tart

Cranberry, Caramel, and Almond Tart

Raspberries on Chocolate

A Bunch of Nuts in a Tart

White Chocolate Cream with Raspberry in a Hazelnut Crust

Figs, Hazelnuts, and Honey

THE TARTS OF FALL AND WINTER

Grapes.

Grapes make me excited that fall has arrived. The first Concord grapes that come to the Greenmarket from the Finger Lakes in upstate New York are my marker for the season. We make Grapes Baked with Hazelnuts, which is one of my favorite tarts of all. As fall settles in, apples and pears from the Hudson Valley fill the farmers' stands and color the market shades of green and gold and crimson. We have more than thirty varieties of apples from which to choose, while the local pears we get are Bartletts, Bosc, Clapp, and Seckels. We use the Bartletts for Square Pear Peg Tarts and White Chocolate Infused with Pear Skins, both of which are unique, simple, and delicious. When the local supply of apples and pears fades, the Greenmarket farmers begin to pack up for the season. With fruit supplies low, we eat our way through the balance of the winter with variations in chocolate and custard tarts. It's not a bad way to deal with the New York City cold.

An "orange tart" gets "made out of apples" because orange zest is infused into a cream and sugar base for the filling. As the tart bakes, the apples absorb the cream coating, and they come out of the oven tasting like oranges.

ORANGE TART MADE OUT OF APPLES

½ cup granulated sugar

1 large orange

½ cup plus 2 tablespoons heavy cream

3 medium Granny Smith or Golden Delicious apples, peeled, cored, and cut into 12 slices each

6 partially baked tart shells (see note), made with Standard Tart Dough (page 16), rings left on

1) Preheat the oven to 375°F.

2) Place the sugar in a medium bowl and grate the zest of the orange into it. Rub the zest and sugar together between the palms of your hands.

3) Place the orange sugar in a small saucepan, add the cream, and heat over medium heat, stirring gently, until the sugar has dissolved. Remove from the heat, and set aside for 10 minutes to infuse. Then strain into a bowl.

4) Put the apples in a bowl, add half of the orange cream, and toss to coat well.

5) Place the tart shells on a baking sheet lined with parchment paper. Arrange 3 apple slices around the sides of each tart shell, and stack 3 slices in the center. Spoon the remaining orange cream over the tarts.

6) Bake for 20 to 25 minutes, until the fruit is golden and the cream is bubbling slowly around the edges. Remove from the oven and let sit for 30 seconds, then remove the tart rings with tongs. Using a wide spatula, transfer to a wire rack to cool for at least 15 minutes before serving.

working note: If using tart pans, leave the partially baked shells in the pans. Cool the baked tarts in the pans on a wire rack for at least 15 minutes, then unmold.

serving note: Even if you want to serve this warm from the oven—it's very good that way—let it cool at least 15 minutes, to give the sides time to firm up.

MAKES 6 TARTS

To me, the single best gauge of a bakery's quality is its lemon tart. It's not a difficult tart to make, but there's a challenge in balancing the sourness of the lemon, the sweet edge of the sugar, and the creaminess of the butter. This recipe produces a delicate, even flavor, and here are four different ways to present it: in the standard tart pastry; in the chocolate crust, where the flavors become more complex; in mini-tart shells; and as part of the most dramatic lemon meringue tart you'll ever meet (see page 76).

LEMON TART, FOUR WAYS

Grated zest of 1 lemon (see step 1)

½ cup freshly squeezed lemon juice

1 cup granulated sugar

4 large eggs

1 large egg yolk

12 tablespoons unsalted butter, cut into 6 pieces

6 fully baked tart shells, made with Standard Tart Dough (page 16) or Chocolate Tart Dough (page 22), or 34 2¼-inch mini-tart shells, made with either dough

1 ounce bittersweet chocolate, melted, for design, or cocoa powder, for dusting

1) Place the sugar in a medium bowl and grate the zest of the lemon into it. Rub the zest and sugar together between the palms of your hands.

2) Strain the lemon juice into a medium nonreactive saucepan. Add the eggs, egg yolk, butter, and the zested sugar, and whisk to combine. Set the pan over medium heat and cook, whisking constantly, for 3 to 5 minutes, until the mixture begins to thicken. Be sure to whisk all over the bottom of the pan, especially the edges. At the first sign of a boil, remove from the heat and strain into a bowl.

3) With a ladle or a large spoon, fill the tart shells with the lemon cream. Refrigerate for 30 minutes, or until set. To fill mini-tart shells, transfer the lemon cream to a small glass, and pour the filling into the shells.

4) Fill a paper pastry bag (see page 24) with the melted chocolate, if using, and stripe and dot each tart or mini-tart to make a simple design, or dust the tops with cocoa powder. Let sit at room temperature for 10 minutes before serving.

MAKES 6 TARTS OR 34 MINI-TARTS

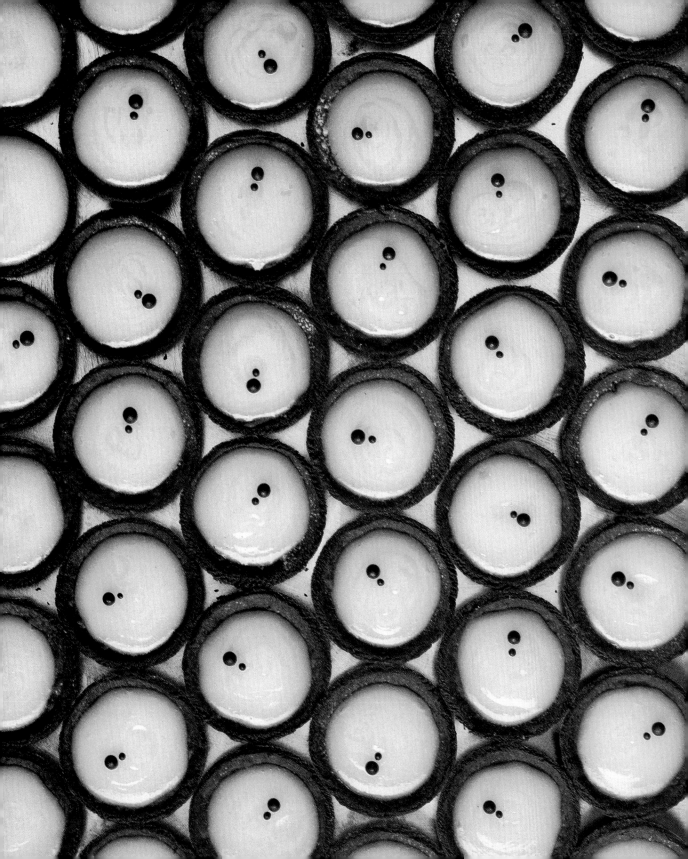

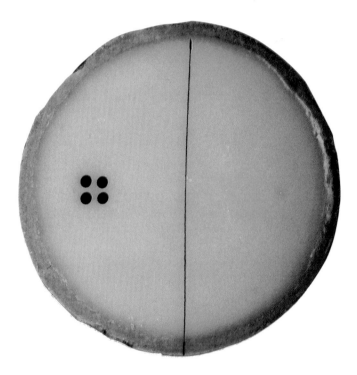

This is a case of stylish engineering with egg whites. You need six small entremet rings to serve as molds to form the meringue. These rings, which come in a variety of sizes, are more commonly used in French bakeries as molds in which to assemble cakes. You can find them in specialty cookware stores or through mail-order sources (see page 107).

LEMON MERINGUE TART, MANHATTAN STYLE

Canola oil or vegetable oil for the rings

6 Lemon Tarts made with Standard Tart Dough (page 72)

6 large egg whites, at room temperature

1 teaspoon cream of tartar

1 cup granulated sugar

6 entremet rings, 3 inches in diameter and 1½ inches high

1) Lightly oil the inside of each entremet ring. Center a ring on top of each tart, and set aside.

2) Place the egg whites in the bowl of a stand mixer or a large mixing bowl. Using the whisk attachment or a hand-held mixer, beat on low speed for 2 minutes. Add the cream of tartar, increase the speed to medium, and beat until soft peaks have formed. Gradually add the sugar in a steady stream, and continue beating until stiff, glossy peaks have formed.

3) Spoon the meringue into the entremet rings, spreading it evenly over the tops of the tarts. Then dip the spoon into the meringue and quickly pull it up to create a small flourish on top of each tart.

4) Place the tarts in the freezer for at least 20 minutes or up to 4 hours.

5) To remove the entremet rings, gently shimmy them back and forth while sliding them up off the meringue. Let the tarts sit at room temperature for 10 minutes before serving.

MAKES 6 TARTS

By infusing this custard with more than one element, you create a layered effect of flavors. You'll taste chocolate, banana, orange, and coconut, then back to chocolate as the flavors evolve in your mouth.

TROPICAL CHOCOLATE TART

1⅓ cups heavy cream

Peel of 1 very ripe banana, coarsely chopped

¼ cup unsweetened shredded coconut

Grated zest of ½ orange (see step 1)

3 large egg yolks

5 ounces bittersweet chocolate, finely chopped

6 fully baked tart shells, made with Chocolate Tart Dough (page 22)

1 ounce bittersweet chocolate, melted, for design

1) Combine the cream, banana peel, and coconut in a large saucepan. Grate the zest of the orange into the cream, and whisk to combine. Bring to a simmer over medium heat, whisking occasionally. Remove from the heat and let cool, whisking occasionally.

2) Strain the coconut cream into a medium saucepan, pressing firmly with the back of a spoon to extract all the flavor from the fruits.

3) Place the egg yolks in a medium bowl.

4) Bring the cream to a simmer. Remove from the heat, and add the chocolate. Let sit for 1 minute, then whisk until smooth. Pour the chocolate cream slowly into the egg yolks, whisking constantly. Strain into a bowl.

5) With a ladle or a large spoon, fill the tart shells with the chocolate cream. Refrigerate for 45 minutes, or until set.

6) Fill a small paper pastry bag (see page 24) with the melted chocolate. Stripe and dot the top of each tart to make a simple design. Let sit at room temperature for 10 minutes before serving.

MAKES 6 TARTS

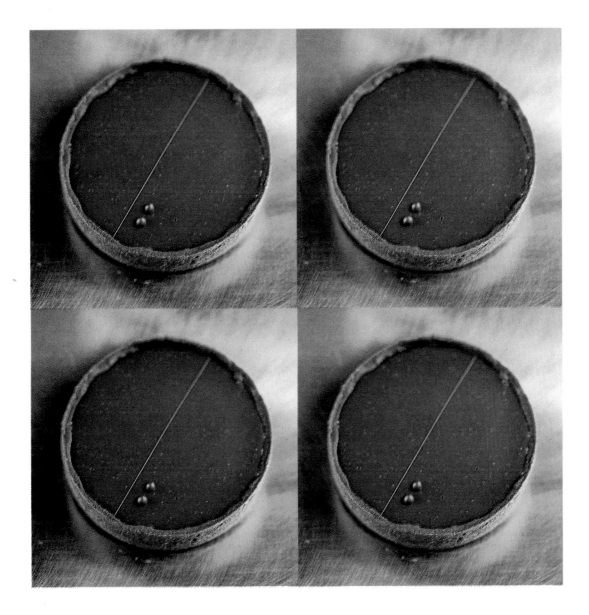

This wasn't always the name: Originally the "peg" was round, not square, but everyone thought that it looked like a nipple and that the tart was supposed to be a breast. This caused a minor commotion, so we changed the shape and renamed it. Looks aside, I love the way this tastes. The texture is luscious and the pear flavor is delicate and clear. Somehow, it tastes floral.

SQUARE PEAR PEG TART

2 large ripe Bartlett or Comice pears

1 cup bottled pear juice

⅓ cup heavy cream

6 fully baked tart shells, made with Standard Tart Dough (page 16)

About 2 tablespoons granulated sugar

1) Peel the pears, slice them lengthwise in half, and remove the cores. Wrap 1 pear half in plastic wrap and refrigerate. Place the other 3 pear halves in a shallow saucepan, add the pear juice, and bring to a simmer. Cook until the fruit is tender and a paring knife can be inserted without resistance, about 10 to 15 minutes.

2) With a slotted spoon, transfer the pears to a bowl, and discard the poaching liquid. Let cool.

3) Place the pears in a food processor or blender and puree until smooth. Transfer to a medium bowl.

4) Pour the cream into a small bowl. Using a hand-held electric mixer, beat at medium speed until very stiff peaks form. Fold the whipped cream into the pear puree.

5) Spoon the pear cream into the tart shells. Gently shake them to level the tops.

6) Cut six ½-inch-square "pegs" from the reserved pear half. Plant 1 peg in the center of each tart. Refrigerate for 15 minutes, or until set.

7) To caramelize the tarts, sprinkle about ½ teaspoon of sugar over the top of each tart, including the pear peg. Using a propane torch, keeping the nozzle of the torch about 4 inches from the top of the tart, circle the flame over the top of each tart until the sugar melts. Sprinkle another ½ teaspoon of sugar over each tart and caramelize the sugar with the torch. Refrigerate for 15 minutes before serving.

working note: I use a propane torch to caramelize the topping as the tart cannot withstand the heat of a broiler.

MAKES 6 TARTS

Fine French pastry meets the American vending machine: creamy milk chocolate on top, a layer of caramel below. Just like the candy bar.

MILKY WAY TART

3½ ounces milk chocolate, finely chopped

1⅓ cups heavy cream

for the caramel:

½ cup heavy cream

4 tablespoons unsalted butter

½ cup plus 2 tablespoons granulated sugar

6 fully baked tart shells, made with Chocolate Tart Dough (page 22)

1 ounce bittersweet chocolate, melted, for design

1) Place the milk chocolate in a medium bowl. Pour the cream into a small saucepan and bring to a boil over medium heat. Pour the hot cream all at once on top of the milk chocolate. Let sit for 1 minute, then whisk until smooth. Strain into a bowl, cover with plastic wrap, and puncture several holes in it with the tip of a paring knife. Refrigerate for at least 4 hours, or overnight.

2) To make the caramel, combine the cream and butter in a small saucepan, and heat over low heat, stirring occasionally, until the butter melts. Remove from the heat.

3) Meanwhile, put the sugar in a large saucepan, and heat over low heat until the sugar melts and turns into a sheet of golden caramel.

4) Immediately whisk the hot cream mixture into the caramelized sugar. The mixture will boil and rise up in the pot. Turn the heat off, and whisk until any hardened pieces of caramel dissolve. Strain into a bowl, and refrigerate for at least 1 hour, until just semisoft.

5) Divide the caramel among the tart shells, spreading it into a 2-inch circle in the center of each one. Set aside.

6) Pour the chilled milk chocolate cream into the bowl of a stand mixer or a medium mixing bowl. Using the whisk attachment or a hand-held mixer, beat at medium speed until medium to firm peaks begin to form. Spoon the whipped chocolate cream into the tarts. Gently shake the tarts to level the tops. Refrigerate for 10 minutes.

7) Fill a small paper pastry bag (see page 24) with the melted chocolate. Stripe and dot the top of each tart. Let sit for 5 to 10 minutes.

MAKES 6 TARTS

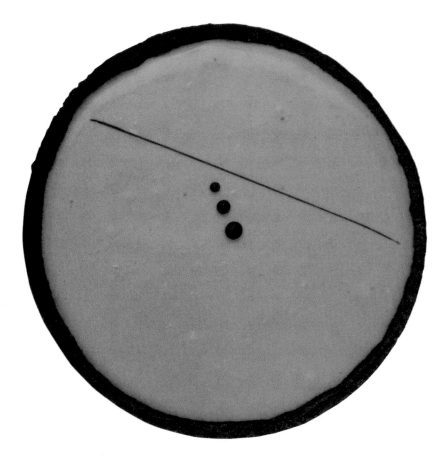

Delicious, but very rich. Don't eat more than one of these at a time.

BANANA CHOCOLATE CHUNK TART

⅓ cup granulated sugar
½ cup heavy cream
4 ripe bananas, cut into 1-inch triangular pieces
3 ounces bittersweet chocolate, cut into pieces roughly ¼ inch by 1 inch
6 partially baked tart shells (see note), made with Chocolate Tart Dough (page 22), rings left on

1) Preheat the oven to 375°F.

2) Combine the sugar and cream in a small saucepan and heat over medium heat, stirring gently, until the sugar has dissolved. Remove from the heat and let cool.

3) Combine the bananas and chocolate in a medium bowl. Add ½ cup of the cream mixture and toss gently to coat the fruit well.

4) Divide the banana mixture among the tart shells, mounding it in the centers. Pour the remaining cream over the tarts.

5) Bake for 20 to 25 minutes until the juices are bubbling slowly around the edges. Remove from the oven and let sit for 30 seconds, then remove the tart rings with tongs. Using a wide spatula, transfer to a wire rack to cool completely.

working note: If using tart pans, leave the partially baked shells in the pans. Cool the baked tarts in the pans on a wire rack, then unmold.

serving note: Sometimes this tart looks great, sometimes, not so great. If the bananas render too much liquid while they bake, it creates a cloudy glaze over the tart that's not so attractive—but even if the look of the tarts may be suspect, the flavor definitely isn't.

MAKES 6 TARTS

This chocolate mousse has no eggs, which is unusual. In fact, I'm not sure it qualifies as real mousse. I used to make a traditional chocolate mousse, separating the eggs, combining the yolks and melted chocolate, whipping the whites until foamy. But when the bakery first opened, I began using new milk and cream from a small farm in upstate New York. The cream was so rich that it threw the mousse recipe out of whack. While adjusting the proportions and retesting, I realized that cream by itself is enough to support the chocolate.

CHOCOLATE MOUSSE TART

1) Place the chocolate in a large bowl.

2) Combine the milk and 3 tablespoons of the cream in a saucepan and bring to a boil over medium heat. Pour the hot milk mixture all at once on top of the chocolate. Let sit for 1 minute, then whisk until smooth. Let cool to room temperature.

3) Pour the remaining ½ cup cream into a mixing bowl. Using a hand-held mixer, beat at medium speed just until soft peaks form. Gently fold half of the whipped cream into the chocolate cream, then fold in the remaining whipped cream.

4) With a ladle or a large spoon, fill the tart shells with the chocolate mousse. Refrigerate for at least 1 hour, or until set.

5) Fill a small paper pastry bag (see page 24) with the melted chocolate. Stripe and dot the top of each tart to make a simple design. Let sit at room temperature for 5 minutes before serving.

working note: This is positively simple to make, but one warning: You must not overwhip the cream. The mousse should be almost pourable. This is not at all standard for chocolate mousse, but it's the way to make this one work.

MAKES 6 TARTS

4 ounces bittersweet chocolate, finely chopped
⅓ cup milk
½ cup plus 3 tablespoons heavy cream
6 fully baked tart shells, made with Chocolate Tart Dough (page 22)
1 ounce bittersweet chocolate, melted, for design

85

Passion fruit has a tart edge, and a passion fruit dessert should have one too. This tart gives you tang that's true to its source, along with some built-in sweet (via raspberry preserves) to help tame it. Design-wise, this was the first-born of City Bakery tarts. When I developed it, its strong geometry and simple beauty really struck me. The spare designs of all of the other tarts followed.

PASSION FRUIT TART WITH A RASPBERRY POLKA DOT

1⅓ cup pure passion fruit juice (see note)

½ vanilla bean, split

3 large egg yolks

¼ cup granulated sugar

½ cup heavy cream

6 fully baked tart shells, made with Standard Tart Dough (page 16)

¼ cup seedless raspberry preserves

1) Fill a large saucepan with 2 to 3 inches of water and bring to a boil.

2) Pour the passion fruit juce into a medium sacuepan, and scrape in the seeds from the vanilla bean and add the pod too. Set the pan over low heat a minute or so until hot.

3) Combine the egg yolks and sugar in a medium metal bowl, and whisk to combine. Set the bowl over the saucepan of boiling water; the bottom of the bowl must not touch the water. Whisk the egg yolks and sugar vigorously until thick and pale and the whisk leaves a trail in the mixture, about 2 minutes. Be sure to whisk all over the bottom and sides of the bowl.

4) Pour the hot passion fruit juice slowly into the egg yolk mixture, whisking constantly. Then, using a wooden spoon, stir until the mixture has thickened and coats the back of the spoon, about 1 minute. Strain through a fine sieve into a large bowl, and let cool.

5) Pour the cream into a mixing bowl. Using a whisk hand-held mixer, beat at medium speed until stiff peaks form. Fold the whipped cream into the cooled passion fruit mixture.

6) Ladle or spoon the passion fruit cream into the tart shells. Freeze for at least 4 hours, or overnight.

7) To make the "polka dots," hold a frozen tart with your fingertips, and insert an apple corer into the passion fruit cream down to the tart shell. Twist and pull the corer out, leaving a cylindrical hole in the tart. Repeat with the remaining frozen tarts.

8) Put the raspberry preserves in a bowl and whisk until smooth. Fill a medium paper pastry bag (see page 24) with the preserves, cut a small opening in the tip, and fill the holes in the tarts with the preserves.

9) Refrigerate for 30 minutes to allow the passion fruit and the preserves to come to the same temperature, then let sit at room temperature for 15 minutes before serving.

ingredient note: Pure passion fruit juice means just that. Passion fruit beverages containing water or alcohol or other juice blends will not work. See page 107 for mail-order sources.

working note: Creating the "polka dot" takes practice. If only part of the passion fruit cylinder comes out with the corer, chisel the rest out with the tip of a small knife.

MAKES 6 TARTS

In a perfect world, Concord grapes would be seedless, and I could bake with them. They're not, so I had accepted the fact that a great grape tart would never be. Then one day, Eileen Farnan of Buzzard Crest Vineyards brought the most delicious organic seedless grapes to the Greenmarket. Not Concords, but Himrods, Canadice, and Niagaras—varietal grapes grown in the Finger Lakes region of New York State. They come from a harvest so small that we get only enough to make these tarts for a week or two each year. You don't need to use special varietal grapes at home, but try to find organic grapes from small growers.

GRAPES BAKED WITH HAZELNUTS

⅓ cup plus 1 tablespoon granulated sugar
½ cup plus 2 tablespoons heavy cream
10 ounces seedless green grapes, stemmed (approximately ¾ cup)
10 ounces seedless red grapes, stemmed (approximately ¾ cup)
3 ounces hazelnuts (approximately ⅔ cup), coarsely chopped
6 partially baked tart shells (see note), made with Standard Tart Dough (page 16), rings left on

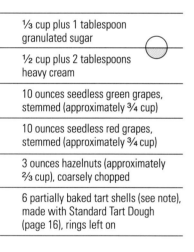

1) Preheat the oven to 375°F.

2) Combine the sugar and cream in a small saucepan and heat over medium heat, stirring gently, until the sugar has dissolved. Remove from the heat and let cool for 10 minutes.

3) Combine the grapes and hazelnuts in a medium bowl. Add half of the cream mixture, and toss to coat.

4) Divide the grape mixture among the tart shells (still in their rings), mounding it in the centers. Pour the remaining cream mixture over the tarts.

5) Bake for 20 to 25 minutes, until the juices are bubbling slowly around the edges. Remove from the oven and let sit for 30 seconds, then remove the tart rings with tongs. Let sit for 10 minutes to allow the sides to firm up, then use a wide spatula to transfer the tarts to a wire rack to cool.

working notes: 1) The results you get depend on the ability of the grapes you use to burst open in the oven, letting their juices cook down. Try to find thin-skinned grapes; green grapes seem to have thinner skins than red grapes, and if you can't find thin-skinned red grapes, it's better to choose grapes that will give the best results instead of insisting on the pleasing contrast of two grape colors. **2)** If using tart pans, leave the partially baked shells in the pans. Cool the baked tarts in the pans on a wire rack, then unmold.

MAKES 6 TARTS

This may sound a little extreme to some people, but at certain times, with certain foods, you should not talk while you are eating. Whether it's taste, texture, or the bouquet of a great glass of wine, sometimes food and drink deserve total concentration. I think this tart is in that category. The pear skin flavor is both subtle and delayed. Wait for it, quietly.

WHITE CHOCOLATE INFUSED WITH PEAR SKINS

1¼ cups heavy cream
Peels from 2 large ripe Bartlett pears
4 ounces white chocolate, finely chopped
6 fully baked tart shells, made with Standard Tart Dough (page 16) or Chocolate Tart Dough (page 22)
1 ounce bittersweet chocolate, melted, for design

1) Combine ¾ cup of the cream and the pear skins in a small saucepan, and bring to a simmer over medium heat. Transfer to a bowl, cover with plastic wrap, and puncture several holes in it with the tip of a paring knife. Refrigerate for at least 4 hours, or overnight.

2) Place the white chocolate in a medium bowl. Pour the remaining ½ cup cream into a small saucepan and bring to a boil over medium heat. Pour the hot cream all at once onto the white chocolate. Let stand for 1 minute, then whisk until smooth. Let cool to room temperature.

3) Strain the chilled pear-infused cream into a mixing bowl, pressing hard with the back of a spoon to extract all of the flavor from the pear skins. Using a hand-held mixer, beat at medium speed just until soft peaks form. Fold the whipped cream into the cooled white chocolate cream.

4) Ladle or spoon the white chocolate cream into the tart shells. Refrigerate for 30 minutes, or until set.

5) Fill a small paper pastry bag (see page 24) with the melted chocolate. Stripe and dot the top of each tart to make a simple design. Let sit at room temperature for 15 minutes before serving.

working note: It is important that the cream not be whipped beyond soft peaks. After the cream has been folded into the white chocolate cream, the mixture should still be almost pourable.

MAKES 6 TARTS

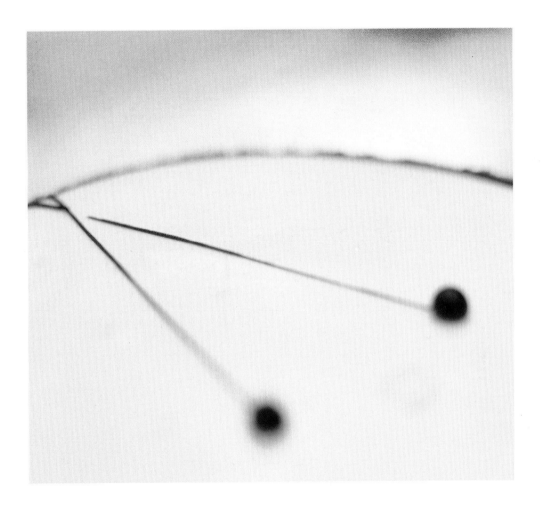

Not a law firm.

PEAR, PINEAPPLE, AND PEPPER

¼ cup granulated sugar

⅔ cup heavy cream

2 medium Bartlett pears

Juice of ½ lemon

¼ ripe pineapple

¼ teaspoon coarsely ground white pepper or black pepper

6 partially baked tart shells (see note), made with Cracked Pepper Tart Dough (page 20), rings left on

1) Preheat the oven to 375°F.

2) Combine the sugar and cream in a medium saucepan, and heat over medium heat, stirring gently, until the sugar has dissolved. Remove from the heat.

3) Peel the pears, slice lengthwise in half, and core. Cut them into 1-inch long triangular shapes, and place in a medium bowl. Toss with the lemon juice.

4) Peel the pineapple and cut it into pieces the same size as the pear. Add to the pears, then add the cream, pepper, and toss to coat.

5) Place the tart shells on a baking sheet lined with parchment paper. Fill the shells with the pears and pineapple, mounding the fruit in the centers. If there's any cream mixture remaining in the bottom of the bowl pour over the tops of the tarts.

6) Bake for 25 to 30 minutes, until the fruit is slightly browned on the tips and the juices are bubbling slowly around the edges of the tarts. Remove from the oven and let sit for 30 seconds, then remove the tart rings with tongs. Using a wide spatula, transfer to a wire rack to cool.

working note: If using tart pans, leave the partially baked shells in the pans. Cool the baked tarts in the pans on a wire rack, then unmold.

MAKES 6 TARTS

This is super easy. Besides making the chocolate chips, which are really chocolate dots, the only thing to do is whip some cream. The mint flavor, which comes from distilled peppermint oil, is subject to your approval. If you don't like mint, substitute orange, berry, or any flavor that goes well with cream and chocolate. You can find a wide range of flavored essences and oils in health food stores or specialty food and spice shops. Just be sure that they are *edible*, and that you use them with a light hand.

MINT CHOCOLATE CHIP TART

2 ounces bittersweet chocolate, melted	
1¼ cups heavy cream	
2 to 3 drops distilled peppermint oil or oil of your choice	
6 fully baked tarts, made with Chocolate Tart Dough (page 22)	

1) To make the chocolate chips, line 2 or 3 baking sheets with parchment paper. Fill 2 or 3 small paper pastry bags (see page 24) with the melted chocolate. Cut a small opening in the tip of one, and set the others aside in a warm place. Pipe out rows of chocolate dots between ¼ inch to ½ inch in diameter, leaving a ¼ inch space between them. Place in the freezer for at least 1 hour.

2) Pour the cream into the bowl of a stand mixer or a mixing bowl. Using the whisk attachment or a hand-held mixer, beat at medium speed until soft peaks begin to form. Add the peppermint oil. With a paring knife or a miniature spatula, scrape most of the frozen chocolate chips onto the cream; do not touch them with your hands, or they will melt. Fold the chips into the cream, and return the remaining chips to the freezer.

3) With a spoon, fill the tart shells with the mint cream. Gently shake the tarts to level the cream tops. Scrape the remaining chips onto the tops of the tarts, and serve.

MAKES 6 TARTS

Crème brûlée is routinely baked in ramekins in a water bath. Since a tart shell cannot sit surrounded by water, the method I use here, adapted from a recipe in <u>Desserts</u> by Nancy Silverton, is to blind-bake the tart shell, then cook the custard separately over boiling water. This requires prolonged rapid whisking to foam the egg yolks while keeping them from curdling. The custard is then ladled into the tart shells and refrigerated to set.

Caramelizing a crème brûlée tart also requires a different approach. Whereas the ramekin version can be caramelized under a broiler, a tart cannot withstand that degree of heat, so you must use a propane torch.

VANILLA BEAN CRÈME BRÛLÉE TART

1½ cups heavy cream
1 vanilla bean, split
4 large egg yolks
¾ cup plus 2 tablespoons granulated sugar
6 fully baked tart shells, made with Standard Tart Dough (page 16) or Chocolate Tart Dough (page 22)

1) Pour the cream into a medium saucepan, and scrape the seeds from the vanilla bean into it. Add the bean. Bring just to a simmer over low heat. Remove from the heat.

2) Meanwhile, fill a large saucepan with 2 to 3 inches of water and bring to a boil over high heat.

3) Combine the egg yolks and 2 tablespoons of the sugar in a medium heatproof bowl, and whisk to combine. Set the bowl over the saucepan of boiling water; the bottom of the bowl must not touch the water. Whisk the yolks and sugar vigorously until thick and pale, and the whisk leaves a trail in the mixture. Be sure to whisk all over the bottom and sides of the bowl.

4) Slowly pour the hot cream into the egg yolk mixture, whisking constantly. Then, using a wooden spoon, stir until the custard has thickened and coats the back of the spoon, approximately 3 to 5 minutes. Strain through a fine sieve into a bowl.

5) With a ladle or a large spoon, fill the tart shells with the custard. Refrigerate for at least 1 hour, or until set.

6) To caramelize the tarts, sprinkle 1 tablespoon of sugar over each tart, and gently shake the tart to distribute the sugar evenly, without lifting it off the work surface. Using a propane torch, keeping the nozzle of the propane torch about 4 inches from the top of the tart, circle the flame over the top of each tart until the sugar has melted. Sprinkle another tablespoon of sugar over each tart and circle the flame over the top until the sugar bubbles and caramelizes. Refrigerate for 10 minutes before serving.

MAKES 6 TARTS

This is the way to finish a holiday meal on a winter night. Serve these tarts warm from the oven, and pick them up with your hands to eat them.

CRANBERRY, CARAMEL, AND ALMOND TART

1 cup granulated sugar
1¼ cups heavy cream
1¾ cups cranberries
6 ounces sliced almonds
6 partially baked tart shells (see note), made with Standard Tart Dough (page 16), rings left on

1) Preheat the oven to 350°F.

2) To make the caramel, spread the sugar in a large heavy skillet and heat over low heat. Place the cream in a small saucepan over low heat next to the sugar, until the sugar melts into a sheet of even caramel, approximately 5 minutes.

3) Meanwhile, heat the cream over low heat.

4) Whisk the heated cream into the caramel and cook until any large pieces of hardened caramel melt. Strain into a medium bowl, and let cool for 15 minutes.

5) Add the cranberries and almonds to the caramel, and stir to coat.

6) Place the tart shells on a baking sheet lined with parchment paper. Divide the cranberry mixture among the tart shells, mounding it up in the centers.

7) Bake for 20 to 25 minutes, until the cranberries have puckered and the juices are bubbling slowly around the edges. Remove from the oven and let sit for 30 seconds, then remove the rings with tongs. Using a wide spatula, transfer to a wire rack to cool for at least 10 minutes before serving.

working note: If using tart pans, leave the partially baked shells in the pans. Cool the baked tarts in the pans on a wire rack for at least 10 minutes, then unmold.

MAKES 6 TARTS

Raspberries are twice-bearing, so there are two seasons when they're available: The first is springtime, the second is the cusp of autumn—and that's when raspberries matched with thick dark chocolate cream seem appropriate for the cooler weather. Of course, seasonal restrictions need not apply; make this any time of the year, as long as you've got great berries.

RASPBERRIES ON CHOCOLATE

3 ounces bittersweet chocolate, finely chopped
1¼ cups heavy cream
1 pint raspberries
6 fully baked tart shells, made with Chocolate Tart Dough (page 22)
Cocoa powder, for dusting
Confectioners' sugar, for dusting

1) Place the chocolate in a medium bowl. Pour the cream into a small saucepan and bring to a boil over medium heat. Pour the hot cream all at once on top of the chocolate. Let sit for 1 minute, then whisk until smooth. Strain into a bowl, cover with plastic wrap, and puncture several holes in the plastic with the tip of a small knife. Refrigerate for at least 5 hours, or overnight.

2) Place the chilled chocolate cream in a mixing bowl. Using a whisk, whip the chocolate until it is slightly thickened, 15 to 30 seconds.

3) Place 5 raspberries in the bottom of each tart shell and press gently to flatten. Spoon the chocolate cream into the tart shells. Arrange the remaining raspberries in the centers of the tarts, mounding them into small pyramids. Sift a touch of cocoa powder and then confectioners' sugar over each tart, and serve.

MAKES 6 TARTS

It's crazy how good this tastes. Very much like a candy bar, and best with a glass of cold milk.

A BUNCH OF NUTS IN A TART

1 cup heavy cream

⅓ cup honey

¼ cup granulated sugar

3 tablespoons butter

3 cups assorted walnuts, peanuts, and/or almonds

½ cup raisins (optional)

6 partially baked tart shells (see note), made with Standard Tart Dough (page 16) or Chocolate Tart Dough (page 22), rings left on

1) Combine the cream, honey, sugar, and butter in a small saucepan and bring just to a boil over medium heat. Simmer, stirring gently, for exactly 1 minute. Remove from the heat, add the nuts and raisins, and stir to coat.

2) Divide the nut mixture evenly among the tart shells (still in their rings), mounding it in the centers.

3) Bake for 20 to 25 minutes, until the filling is caramelized and bubbling around the edges. Remove from the oven and let sit for 30 seconds, then remove the rings with tongs. Using a wide spatula, transfer to a wire rack to cool.

working notes: 1) Don't let the honey and cream mixture simmer for longer than 1 minute, or the filling will become too hard when it cools and sets. **2)** If using tart pans, leave the partially baked shells in the pans. Cool the baked tarts in the pans on a wire rack, then unmold.

MAKES 6 TARTS

Dreamy-light texture, delicate flavors, and incredibly, admirably fragile.

WHITE CHOCOLATE CREAM WITH RASPBERRY IN A HAZELNUT CRUST

4 ounces white chocolate, finely chopped

1¼ cups heavy cream

1 tablespoon seedless raspberry preserves

6 fully baked tart shells, made with Hazelnut Tart Dough (page 20)

1 ounce bittersweet chocolate, melted, for design

1) Place the white chocolate in a medium bowl.

2) Pour 1 cup of the cream into a small saucepan and bring to a boil over medium heat. Pour the hot cream all at once over the white chocolate. Let sit for 1 minute, then whisk until smooth. Strain into a bowl, cover with plastic wrap, and puncture several holes in it with the tip of a paring knife. Refrigerate for at least 4 hours, or overnight.

3) Divide the raspberry preserves among the tart shells, spreading a thin layer over the bottom of each one.

4) Combine the chilled white chocolate cream and the remaining ¼ cup cream in the bowl of a stand mixer or a mixing bowl. Using the whisk attachment or a hand-held mixer, beat at medium speed until soft peaks form. Spoon the white chocolate cream into the tart shells. Gently shake the tarts to level the tops.

5) Fill a small paper pastry bag (see page 24) with the melted bittersweet chocolate. Stripe and dot the top of each tart, and serve.

working notes: 1) Consider the "incredibly, admirably" fragility a warning! Handle the tart shells with care. **2)** This white chocolate cream is a great resource for pastry professionals to have on hand. Keep a supply of the unwhipped white chocolate cream in the refrigerator, and you'll have the ability to produce desserts on a moment's notice. In fact, the cream is delicious simply mounded on individual plates and garnished with fruit. It holds well for 4 to 5 days.

MAKES 6 TARTS

Sweet and rich, with a little crunch. You can make these flavors even more special by combining them with the right bottle of dessert wine. I recommend Malvasia delle Lipari, an Italian wine that's deep amber in color, full of body, and rich enough to stand up to the flavors of the tart.

FIGS, HAZELNUTS, AND HONEY

½ cup plus 1 tablespoon heavy cream

2 tablespoons honey

18 ripe figs

½ cup hazelnuts, coarsely chopped

6 partially baked tart shells (see note), made with Standard Tart Dough (page 16), rings left on

1) Preheat the oven to 375°F.

2) Combine the cream and honey in a small saucepan, and stir over medium heat until the honey has dissolved. Remove from the heat and set aside for 5 minutes.

3) Meanwhile, slice the figs: Cut large figs into 4 pieces and smaller figs in half.

4) Combine the fruit and hazelnuts in a medium bowl, add half of the honey cream, and gently stir to coat.

5) Divide the fig mixture among the tart shells (still in their rings); do not pack the figs too tightly into the shells. Drizzle the remaining cream over the tarts.

6) Bake for 20 to 25 minutes, until the juices are slowly bubbling around the edges of the tarts. Remove from the oven and let sit for 30 seconds, then remove the rings with tongs. Using a wide spatula, transfer to a wire rack to cool completely.

working note: If using tart pans, leave the partially baked shells in the pans. Cool the baked tarts in the pans on a wire rack, then unmold.

MAKES 6 TARTS

MAIL-ORDER SOURCES

Bridge Kitchenware
214 East 52nd Street
New York, New York 10022
212-688-4220
*Flan rings for the tarts and a wide selection
of other pastry equipment.*

Community Mill and Bean
R.D. 1
Route 89
Savannah, New York 13146
800-755-0554
*This is where we get our organic flour.
Order unbleached white flour, and specify
no wheatgerm.*

Crate & Barrel
725 Landhehr Road
Northbrook, Illinois 60062
800-323-5461 (for nearest store)
A wide selection of pastry equipment.

La Cuisine
323 Cameron Street
Alexandria, Virginia 22314
*Valrhona chocolate and specialty
pastry equipment.*

Dairyland USA
311 Manida Street
Bronx, New York 10474
718-842-8700
*Chocolates, including a wide selection of
Valrhona, Tahitian vanilla beans, and other
specialty pastry ingredients.*

Deep Mountain Maple Syrup
P.O. Box 68
West Glover, Vermont 05875
802-525-4162
My favorite Vermont maple syrup.

Penny's Herb Company & General Store
97 ½ East 7th Street
New York, New York 10009
212-614-0716
Edible flavored essential oils.

J. B. Prince
29 West 38th Street
New York, New York 10018
212-302-8611
*Flan rings and other specialty
pastry equipment.*

Sur la Table
84 Pine Street
Seattle, Washington 98100
206-448-2244
800-240-0853
Flan rings for the tarts.

Vann's Spices
1238 East Joppa Road
Baltimore, Maryland 21286
410-583-1643
Spices and extracts.

Williams-Sonoma
P.O. Box 7456
San Francisco, California 94120-7456
800-541-2233
*Flan rings for the tarts and a wide selection
of pastry equipment.*

INDEX

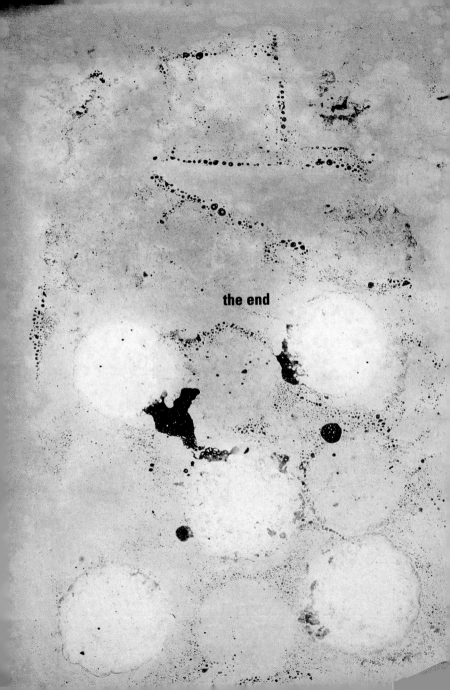

the end